Coping with a Parent Who Overdrinks

EMPOWERING YOU

The Rowman & Littlefield Empowering You series is aimed to help you, as a young adult, deal with important topics that you, your friends, or family might be facing. Whether you are looking for answers about certain illnesses, social issues, or personal problems, the books in this series provide you with the most up-to-date information. Throughout each book you will also find stories from other teenagers to provide personal perspectives on the subject.

Coping with a Parent Who Overdrinks

Insights and Tips for Teenagers

Michelle Shreeve

ROWMAN & LITTLEFIELD

Lanham • Boulder • New York • London

Rowman & Littlefield
Bloomsbury Publishing Inc, 1385 Broadway, New York, NY 10018, USA
Bloomsbury Publishing Plc, 50 Bedford Square, London, WC1B 3DP, UK
Bloomsbury Publishing Ireland, 29 Earlsfort Terrace, Dublin 2, D02 AY28, Ireland
www.rowman.com

British Library Cataloguing in Publication Information Available

Library of Congress Cataloging-in-Publication Data Available

ISBN 978-1-5381-7767-9 (pbk : alk. paper)
ISBN 978-1-5381-7768-6 (ebook)

For product safety related questions contact productsafety@bloomsbury.com.

∞™ The paper used in this publication meets the minimum requirements of American
National Standard for Information Sciences—Permanence of Paper for Printed Library
Materials, ANSI/NISO Z39.48-1992.

To God, Chris, and Johnny. I love you three
more than you will ever know.

To my late mother Kathy, my father Dave,
and my brother Mike. I love you.

To all families affected by overdrinking. May the love you
have for one another get you through the hard days that
come with parental overdrinking. May lost time come
back through healing for all members of your family.

CONTENTS

Acknowledgments

Many thanks go out to those involved in the production of this book. I would like to thank God, Chris, Johnny, Kathy, Dave, Mike, the Library of Congress, the Apache Junction Library, Jon Weeks, Jim Gigliotti, Wendy Gigliotti, Christine Gigliotti, Joe Gigliotti, Jan Gigliotti, Ed Gigliotti, Carmela Gigliotti, Judy Lincicum, Terry Shreeve, Heather and Josh, Cheryl Shreeve, Debbie Casey, Kathy Esquivel, Renee Hanke, Evan Chelini, Ed Chelini, Dottie Chelini, Cody Jenkins, Chris Kane, Stacy Nadzan, the Angeloff Family, Christen Karniski, Joanna Wattenberg, and the folks at Rowman & Littlefield, Jody Lamb, Megan, Sarah, Dilek, Skeeter, Georgianne, Ava, Veronica, Don Dailey Jr., Dr. Marlen Elliot Harrison, *The AutoEthnographer* magazine, Times New Media Publications, Paul Maryniak, Tony Ramseyer, Vicky Camacho, Chris Putman, Al-Anon, Alateen, Andrea Laneri-Martin, Corpus Christi Catholic Church, and Monica Torres.

Introduction

DEAR READER. I AM SO GLAD THAT YOU FOUND THIS BOOK. If you found this book, chances are you might be hiding a big secret—or perhaps maybe you are not. Maybe your family knows, but possibly your friends do not. Maybe your counselor knows, but your teachers do not. What matters the most is that *you* know. You know that you have one or two parents who overdrink in your household. With this challenge comes lots of hard days, confusing days, angry days, and sad days. Especially if you are keeping this secret alone. You are brave, but also heartbroken. You love your parent, but at times you might feel like you resent them. You try to understand why, and every day can feel like an emotionally confusing roller-coaster ride. If you have been keeping this a secret, surely you have your reasons. With that being said, that also means you have been trying to cope with your secret alone, and I am here to tell you that you are not alone. You do not have to walk this alone anymore.

Again, I am glad you found this book. Let it help guide you along this incredibly stressful journey. Please hold on to the words throughout these pages, especially the words from others your age who are going through this or have gone through this already, and let it reassure you that you are not alone, you have never been alone, and you will never be alone.

AUTHOR NOTE

A note before you start reading. Throughout the book, I have sprinkled context about certain scenes from movies that depict alcoholism and overdrinking parents. I mention the movie and the scene that pertains to overdrinking only, and I do not analyze and break down all of the other messages that might be depicted throughout these movies. Some of you readers are age eighteen and over, while others might be under eighteen. If you are under eighteen, double-check with your parent or guardian first before/ if you decide to watch these movies to further explore the context that I share to make sure they want you to learn about other messages in these listed movies. Again, I am only touching on the parts of the movies that pertain to overdrinking to help provide you, the reader, a little more relatable context into what might be going on in your personal life. I am in no way encouraging or discouraging the other messages in these movies.

We learn through repetition. The more we say something to ourselves over and over, the more we will believe it. You will read a lot in this book about things that I mention more than once—that you are not alone, that you should reach out to a trusted adult for help and guidance, and more. The repetition is not there to annoy you—it is strategically written throughout this book to help guide you on your especially hard days, when you think you have no one to turn to or that you have to face this alone. In those moments while you are turning to these chapters, I am trying to help you remember that you have plenty of options to turn to— hence, these options are repeated.

Also, this book is written for *you*. The one who is currently trying to navigate one or two overdrinking parents at home. This book is not written to try and uncover the real reasons behind your parent's (or parents') overdrinking behavior. Upon researching this subject yourself, you will come across many scientific papers, academic journals, organizations, rehab centers, studies conducted, psychologists, psychiatrists, doctors, and more saying that overdrinking is a brain disorder, an addiction, an illness, that the overdrinker is in control, that their overdrinking is out of their control, that it is caused by a traumatic event, that your parent started overdrinking because of peer pressure when they turned twenty-one, that they started overdrinking because it's in their family history, and so much more. I could write a whole other book just based on the potential causes behind your parent's overdrinking and the science and research behind it. I touch on this lightly throughout this book to give you context into the chemical aspect of why your overdrinking parent is lashing out at you while they are intoxicated, for example, to provide you some insight, but again, that is not the focus of this book. *And I am not choosing sides as to the cause of overdrinking is a choice versus addiction.* Each overdrinking parent is different than the next overdrinking parent and will have different circumstances that need to be factored in than the next. Same with how each one of you readers has a different situation and circumstances than the next. There is no one-size-fits-all answer or reasoning behind this. The focus of this book is helping *you* cope and navigate this situation by offering resources and tips on seeking out support and helping *you* not feel alone by sharing the stories of others your age in similar situations, and more. This book is about helping *you* rather than explaining the science behind what is causing your parent to overdrink in the first place.

Some of these true participant stories might be disturbing, but they are being shared freely and honestly by the participants. Some participants have changed their names to protect their true identities.

Suicide and self-harm are mentioned as well as different types of abuse. Please see the resources section at the end of this book if you are struggling with any of this.

Shall we get started?

WHAT IS LIVING WITH AN OVERDRINKING PARENT?

ACCORDING TO THE MERRIAM-WEBSTER DICTIONARY, THE definition of overdrinking is to drink, especially alcohol, to excess (more than the usual, proper, or specified amount). Well, what is considered the usual, proper, or specified amount? According to the National Institute on Alcohol Abuse and Alcoholism (NIAAA; a US federal government agency that has been around for more than fifty years that researches alcoholism and its effects), drinking in moderation translates to two drinks or less in a day for men, and one drink or less in a day for women.[1] According to the Substance Abuse and Mental Health Services Administration (SAMHSA; a branch of the US Department of Health and Human Services for over thirty years), binge drinking, or drinking with the aim of getting drunk, translates to five or more alcoholic drinks for males or four or more alcoholic drinks for females on the same occasion (at the same time or within a couple of hours of each other) on at least one day in the past month.[2] According to the NIAAA, heavy drinking is five or more drinks on any day or fifteen or more per week for men, and consuming four or more on any day or eight or more drinks per week for women.[3] According to *Britannica*, a drink, in this case an alcoholic beverage, is any fermented liquor, such as wine, beer, or distilled spirits, that contains ethyl alcohol, or ethanol (CH_3CH_2OH), as an intoxicating agent.[4]

So, based on the information you just read, does your parent or both parents drink in moderation, binge drink, or do they drink heavily? Overdrinking would mean they drink more than in moderation, more than what is healthy and recommended. In other words, does your father drink more than two drinks in a day? If so, then he is overdrinking. Does your mother drink more than one drink in a day? If so, then she is overdrinking. And then there are the extra circumstances of how your parent's behavior changes when they drink. Do they put you down? Say hurtful things to you? Neglect to take care of you? Are they financially irresponsible, buying beer more than stocking the pantry with food for you? Do you get embarrassed by their drunken behavior in public places? Do your parents fight a lot at home due to overdrinking?

Think about it for a second, and you will know if you have an overdrinking parent. Just remember that you cannot base the ideas or facts as to whether or not you indeed have an overdrinking parent at home based on directly asking your overdrinking parent this question, as you might not get an honest answer for many reasons.

Throughout this book, we will be using the term "overdrinking" instead of "alcoholic" because some readers are on the fence as to what they categorize their parent as. Living with an overdrinking parent means that your life at home is hard on some days or, for some of you, most days. While your peers have parents who do not drink and their homelives are not sporadic or chaotic, your homelife is different if you have one or two overdrinking parents. While your peers might have positive supportive parents who are loving and encouraging, your overdrinking parent situation might seem like a roller-coaster ride. One second your overdrinking parent is kind and encouraging, the next second they are belittling you in a drunken rage or embarrassing you in front of others while out in public. Living with a parent who overdrinks is a lifestyle you did not ask for or choose. It is the hand you were dealt in life. We cannot always control the hand life deals us, but we can learn how to react in a more positive way to help cope with a situation we may be facing.

Living with an overdrinking parent is a *temporary* situation. You can distance yourself from the situation when you come of age to move out of your house and live with another relative or go out into the world and support yourself. Even if your overdrinking parent stays an overdrinking parent as you enter adulthood, you do not have to live under their roof forever and be stuck in an ongoing negative, toxic situation. You are not alone, and this is not a permanent condition that you will have to deal with for the rest of your life. It is temporary. Although this moment seems like forever, this difficult season in your life will pass.

However, please know, that this does not mean your overdrinking parent will quit drinking. Maybe one day they might, but maybe they never will. We all make choices in life, and we all have to live with the consequences. Your parent might be in the "choice" or the "addiction has taken control over their brain" stage. Yet, you will not be living under your overdrinking parent's roof for the rest of your life. One day, as life always does, it will move you forward, and you will not be living with your overdrinking parent anymore. For now, use this book as a lifeline to help you while you are in this *temporary* situation.

CHAPTER 1

Causes of Overdrinking

APPROXIMATELY 7.5 MILLION US CHILDREN AGES SEVENTEEN and younger live with a parent who has alcohol use disorder.[1] That is just about 10 percent of the US population. That is a lot of children living in households with one or two overdrinking parents. Knowing this fact does not make your situation at home any easier. It might even be more confusing trying to figure out why this is happening in the first place. You might already be poking around news articles on the internet or reaching out to family members to investigate what the root cause of your parent's overdrinking is.

On the internet and while doing your own investigating, you are going to come across many pieces of information that might seem conflicting and confusing to you. Some of your research might reflect that overdrinking is a disease of the brain related to addiction. Other research you come across will focus on saying overdrinking is a choice. Again, this book is focused on *you* the reader, and not solely on the controllable or uncontrollable motives behind your parent's overdrinking.

Do you know what the driving force behind your parent's overdrinking behavior is? Does it run in your family? Does it go back a few generations? Was it triggered by some devastating event that happened in your parent's life? Do they seem in control of their overdrinking or out of control of their overdrinking? The only person we want to focus on interpreting this is *you*. Everyone around the overdrinking parent including the overdrinking parent themselves is going to give you different answers and different opinions on the situation. This book will help you interpret the situation for yourself. You can look your overdrinking parent square in the face and flat out ask them to be honest with you and tell you that they have an overdrinking problem. Chances are they will deny that they do. Very rarely will they ever admit to having an overdrinking problem. So, then what? Are you supposed to absorb that answer even though you can clearly see the signs of their overdrinking behavior? How is your parent's overdrinking behavior affecting your everyday life? Enough to accept that they don't have an overdrinking problem just because they say they don't? Or enough for you to challenge what they are telling you and disagree with them because you can clearly see otherwise?

A question that might bother you often is why does your parent overdrink? You think of all the possible answers to try and justify their drinking behavior—your mom is stressed from work, or your father likes to drink a lot with his buddies to hang out and have fun, and that's why. This might have some truth to it in some cases, but a lot of times drinking problems originated before you were even born. Most of the time, they are for reasons that have nothing to do with you. The reasons, instead, have everything to do with them. Children of parents who overdrink get feelings of guilt and try to accept blame that they are the reason why their parent overdrinks. Please don't ever think that you are the cause of your parent's overdrinking habits. Unless you are physically forcing your parent to drink, drink after drink, it's not fair for you to ever take that blame. And, if while drunk your parent blames you for their drinking problem, please remember that they are saying that while they are intoxicated. A rule of thumb is to never accept what your parent says to you while they are intoxicated. They aren't thinking clearly, and oftentimes, by the next day or when they are sober, they don't even remember what they said to you. Your parent is an adult who makes their own choices. You should never be blamed, nor should you ever take the blame. It is also not your fault that your parent overdrinks no matter if they try and tell you this or not while they are intoxicated.

Genetics have been proven to play a part in how overdrinking can be passed down through generations. Oftentimes, if a teenager of a parent who overdrinks starts digging through their family's history, they will learn that alcohol didn't just randomly show up with their parent—alcohol has probably been heavily present in at least one other family member's life, and possibly even generations before them. In other cases, a parent's overdrinking tendencies aren't a vicious generational cycle that keeps popping up but, rather, stems from something traumatic, like a really bad car accident, that happened in their childhood, which led them down a path of overdrinking. There are different reasons for each overdrinking parent. In some cases, you may never find out what the real reason is. As hard as this may be, what you should be focusing on is *you* and how to help *yourself* cope and navigate through all of this. Talking to an overdrinking parent and expressing your concerns is a healthy conversation to have, but only with a parent who admits they are an overdrinker. Most parents are going to deny they overdrink at all, and it is very difficult to have such a conversation with someone who does not want to acknowledge they have a problem.

You will come across a lot of information regarding overdrinking parents and their behavior patterns. Some will say they overdrink by choice, while others will say it is a disease or even a genetic disorder. Or all of the above. Each family is different and will have extenuating circumstances to take into account. If you want to learn more about the science and research behind what happens in the brain and body pertaining to overdrinking, see chapter 5.

Whether or not your overdrinking parent has a family history of overdrinking behavior patterns, they still chose to take that very first drink, if you think about it. Over time, the more your parent overdrinks, they can develop an addiction to alcohol, and it will be increasingly difficult for them to stop. But they still chose to take that very first drink—whether it was on their twenty-first birthday, before then, or even after then; didn't they? The addiction they may have now was initially activated by a choice. Over time, their brain might have gotten out of control by alcohol guiding it, but at what point can they choose to get help or enter a rehab program and stop? Or are they choosing to keep drinking? You can go down a rabbit hole of information trying to decipher this, but your energy needs to go toward helping yourself cope at home.

Skeeter Reflecting on Trying to Understand the Cause of Her Father's Overdrinking

I've been dealing with my father's overdrinking habits for many years now. It has been very stressful, emotionally traumatizing, and the most taxing years of my life. I've been up and down with emotions this whole time even to where my father has broken my heart numerous times, has said terrible things to me that he always denies, and has left me with negative memories more than he's given me positive memories. Some days I feel anger toward him and the choices he's made—the overdrinking choices he has made have affected and changed my life in harder ways. Other days I'm just sad from his overdrinking decisions because I always feel like the beer bottle has been more important to him than I ever will be. I think of all the time lost in our relationship.

Just this past year, instead of bouncing back and forth between being sad and angry with him, I tried something new. I wanted to take a high road approach and give him the benefit of the doubt. I wanted to understand the "why" behind his overdrinking. Why does my father overdrink? What's the reason behind it?

My mother died when I was young. At first, I thought that was the reason why my father overdrank. But then I realized that couldn't be the reason because he drank and caused problems while he was married to my mother before she got sick and before she passed away. Then I started thinking more and traced the alcohol back to his father, my grandfather. I don't know much about my grandfather except that he overdrank as well. So, then I went the genetic route thinking my father overdrinks because his father did before him. After all, kids grow up watching and mirroring their parents, right? I took it another step to try to understand why my grandfather overdrank. The only other fact I know about my grandfather was that he was a Marine. Could that have been the reason? Did my grandfather overdrink to cope with what he witnessed from the war? You hear about those who serve in the armed forces coming back from war with PTSD [post-traumatic stress disorder]. Maybe my grandfather came back from the war and used alcohol to cope with what he witnessed while fighting. But then my father witnessed my grandfather drinking and then my father started drinking, too, when he was just a little boy.

I feel like it's just going down a rabbit hole trying to search for clues as I will never know for sure what the real reason is behind my father's overdrinking. I just feel bad because now my older brother overdrinks as he was exposed to my father's overdrinking when he was a kid just like my father was exposed to my grandfather's drinking when he was a kid before him. Now that's three generations in my family that I can trace back to alcohol. It's like a vicious cycle, but will it ever end? Was there a first person in our ancestry who started it all? Who will be the last in our ancestry to stop the cycle?

I made a personal choice a long time ago, when I was younger, to never drink. I didn't want to become like my father and do what he did to me to my future family. I have succeeded in my personal quest thus far, and I am determined to be the first person to break the cycle. However, as far back as I can trace my overdrinking ancestry, it doesn't affect the women ancestors, only the men. So maybe I can't stop the cycle because I am a girl?[2]

Dilek's Story about Her Overdrinking Father

I never felt and I never feel anger or frustration toward my father because of his alcoholism as I knew and now know better that he had serious problems with his own family. He was like a little helpless child for me because he never stopped for a second and thought about himself even in one day. He either worked like crazy or became drunk. This was obviously to forget or ignore a problem.[3]

Georgianne's Story about Her Overdrinking Mother

My mother became an alcoholic after the death of my father when I was nine. She possibly became one after she married an alcoholic. So, my mother and stepfather were both alcoholics. They are both deceased now of course and yes, I had siblings that all grew up having these parents. My two half-brothers became alcoholics.[4]

Sarah's Story of Her Overdrinking Mother

My mother has been an overdrinker my entire life and she still suffers from it. There were many attempts to help her, but none were ever successful because my mom did not have the desire to be sober or recognize her severe problem. She would say that she had a beer because her arthritis was bothering her.[5]

Megan's Story of Her Overdrinking Mother

My father recognized that my mother had an extremely traumatic childhood. When I was an adult, he finally told me stories that my mother had forbidden him from telling me. I'm unsure why she wanted to keep her past so hidden from me because knowing about her life would have been very helpful for me to understand why she fell into the grip of addiction. My mother's father was an extreme alcoholic, and she and her seven siblings grew up in poverty before and after her father passed away from alcoholism when my mother was only eleven years old. There were several traumatic events that marred her childhood and once I knew the full story, it was obvious why my mother fell into addiction. She used alcohol to dull the pain of unresolved trauma. Once you are addicted to alcohol, it is hard to recover from it.

My mother recognized that she was addicted to alcohol but spoke little of it. Every time she did, she was enveloped in shame. My mother attended AA meetings briefly but was never committed to the program, so it was ineffective. For a short stint, she met with a therapist, but as the therapist began asking her to dive into what happened during her childhood, she stopped going to the appointments.[6]

Overdrinking very rarely just pops up out of the blue. Typically, there is family history of overdrinking somewhere along the way. It's sad, because families are negatively impacted at a multigenerational level. In society, science, and even the world of academia, it seems like it is a battle between seeing the overdrinker as the victim or the overdrinker as the victimizer, to the family around the overdrinker as enabling the behavior to continue, and more. It can get confusing for you, the reader, as you are trying to piece together your overdrinking parent's past along with what society, science, and medicine is trying to tell you.

There was a choice made in the very beginning that led to this path, but genetics potentially fueled alcohol consumption, which later led to this addiction. It's easy to say that the overdrinker is the victimizer to everyone else around them, including you, the young reader; however, we have to remember that although it is not fair that you are getting treated poorly, the hard reality is that, chances are, your overdrinking parent could have been victimized themselves by some other family member as a child. And then maybe that family member was victimized as well. It's an unfortunate cycle and it is frustrating for everyone involved.

You may never know the real/true/factual reason why your parent started overdrinking, but one thing is true: whether it's connected to genetics, or their choice of an unhealthy coping method, or an addiction they're struggling with—it is not your fault. There are rehab places everywhere, they can seek out counseling, support groups, and more to help with their over-drinking, but for some reason they might not be choosing to do that. They might think they can't or it's too late, or they simply don't want to or don't feel like they have a problem. It takes a lot of courage and strength for your overdrinking parent to realize they have a problem. It also depends on how long they have been drinking, as that much alcohol over the years might have taken full control of their brain at this point. Which means the only way out for them is to seek professional help.

Movie break: *FLIGHT*

In *Flight*, pilot Whip Whitaker (played by actor Denzel Washington), struggles silently with a drug and alcohol use problem. When a flight he is piloting experiences a severe turbulence problem, Whip, who had passed out because he was drunk from partying the night before, wakes up to his copilot trying to recover from a steep dive the plane is taking. Whip jolts awake and maneuvers the plane to make a con-trolled landing with a few casualties, while saving the major-ity on board. The NTSB (National Transportation Safety Board) investigations performed a drug test on Whip while he was unconscious after he hit his head from the landing. Reports showed he was indeed intoxicated while piloting the plane. One of the flight attendants who died in the crash tested positive for alcohol and Whip can blame her for his actions of drinking with her the night before the crash, which would give him a get out of jail free card. Arriving at a pro-verbial fork in the road, Whip has to decide whether to blame a deceased person or own up and take responsibility for his drinking, no matter what it costs him. He takes the high road and admits to his drinking problem. His admission lands him in prison, in a support group with other inmates, and he tries hard to mend his broken relationship with his son.[7]

With all of the conflicting and confusing information out there, you have to realize it is a personal choice your overdrinking parent has to make to stop the overdrinking. You cannot change them or force them to stop overdrinking or to seek out help for their overdrinking behavior. It is out of your control. They either need a wake-up call to happen, or they need to be their own wake-up call. You are not to blame. It is not your fault. You are not alone. You are not the cause of their overdrinking. It is out of your control. Focus on yourself and your well-being and what you can control.

MOVIE BREAK: *HACKSAW RIDGE*

In *Hacksaw Ridge*, which is based on a true story, Desmond Doss (played by actor Andrew Garfield), has a war veteran father who becomes an abusive alcoholic based on what he witnessed and experienced while serving in World War I. His father verbally and physically abuses his family out of his drunkenness. It makes childhood life difficult and challenging to say the least. The common ground where they finally begin to heal is found when Desmond takes his turn to serve his country and enters World War II as a conscientious objector (a person who refuses to bear arms due to religious beliefs, moral, or ethical grounds), and now needs support from his abusive alcoholic father to make sure that the army respects his personal decision to be a conscientious objector despite the hard time the army gives him about his decision.[8]

SITUATIONAL CAUSES OF OVERDRINKING

In cases where there aren't generational overdrinking patterns, a single event could have triggered your parent to go down this path. A car accident with severe injuries or trauma, a death in the family, job loss, divorce, or other events that could have triggered the choice to start overdrinking. Maybe your parent did not know how to cope with some event that happened to them and so they turned to overdrinking. Again, there is some choice involved in this whole situation. The more your parent continues to over-drink, the more an addiction forms and takes control over their brain and decision-making skills. No matter the cause, if you are reading this book, that means your parent's overdrinking is causing problems either for them personally, or for you witnessing their behavior daily—or both.

CHAPTER 2

Daily Challenges

LIVING WITH A PARENT WHO OVERDRINKS CAN BE CHALLENGING
to say the least. While your peers seem to have normal households, your household's day-to-day might look a little different,
especially if its status is kept a secret from your peers. "The family environment of alcoholics is typically marked by a significant
degree of chaos. Alcoholic families tend to be driven by a system
of rigidity, such as lack of flexibility and arbitrary rules, that pre-
dispose children to develop a sense of overwhelm or confusion.
This response is marked by feelings of fear that remain unex-
pressed or unresolved, which can lead to emotional shutting down
and detachment from loved ones."[1] There are functional and
healthy families, and then there are dysfunctional and unhealthy
families. Which category do you think your household falls in?

Skeeter Discusses Challenges with
Her Overdrinking Father
As a high school student, it's like my father's overdrinking was getting
worse. After my mother died, my father remarried and the woman who
he married tended to overdrink as well. So sometimes my stepmother
would get irritated at my father when he overdrank, and other times I
felt like I had to deal with both of them overdrinking at the same time,
which was hard.

My father liked to eat out at fancy restaurants. He had this rule that I hated. Whenever we would go out to a restaurant there were two conditions: (1) The restaurant had to serve alcohol, or we couldn't pick that restaurant; (2) He had a two-drink minimum. In other words, we couldn't leave the restaurant until he had at least two beers. I can't tell you how many times I needed to get home during the school week to finish my homework and I was forced to stay at a restaurant well after we all finished eating our food just to wait for my father to finish his beers. And when I would try to tell him I still had homework to finish he would get mad if I tried to rush him to finish. He would never chug, but instead would just slowly sip his beers. So if we all finished our dinner within an hour, most households would just pay their bill, get up, and go home. Not my family. We would have to sit there sometimes for two or three hours until after my father finished his last sip. Sometimes he ordered a bottle or can of beer, sometimes a glass of wine, oftentimes it was finishing a bottle of Chianti or a pint of beer or schooner. Since I didn't have a driver's license yet, I was stuck at the restaurant until my father said we could leave. The only relief I had from that was when my older brother finally got his driver's license and then we would take two cars to restaurants and I would leave with my brother, leaving my father and stepmother at the restaurants so they could finish their two-drink minimum rule.

Birthday parties and BBQs were different than my peers'. We always had to have alcohol, even if it was a party for my brother and I . . . the adults always had to have alcohol present at every party.

I can't tell you how much money was spent during my whole childhood on alcohol. Would you believe that it was about twenty years' worth of bills and receipts that most likely would have covered my college tuition costs for my bachelor's degree?

The worst was, for my father's fiftieth birthday party, his goal was to have fifty drinks in a single day. Between hard liquor shots, glasses of wine, beer cans, and bottles, my father surpassed that goal and ended up having around sixty drinks in one day—in front of me and my family and with a bunch of buddies. He felt so accomplished, but I felt so embarrassed that that was his actual goal to complete for his fiftieth birthday.[2]

Ava's Story about Daily Life with Her Overdrinking Mother

My whole childhood was chaotic to say the least. My mom and stepdad fought a lot, we didn't have a lot of money, my mother was there but usually not mentally present and my stepdad also worked a lot. My mom would be home with me and my siblings while my stepdad worked since she usually worked nights in bars or didn't work at all, but she spent a lot of time sleeping or "cleaning," which usually just consisted of her wiping the same surface over and over again. If my mother wasn't sleeping or "cleaning," she was likely yelling at us and/ or just locked herself in her room. I have countless memories of being yelled at for things that had nothing to do with me and anything that bothered me, and if I tried to tell my mom about it, she would turn it into how it bothered her and she would dismiss my feelings. I was yelled at a lot for being a terrible kid and often felt like it was better to just sit still and be quiet. I enjoyed school a lot, and as a kid I thought that was just because I was smart and did well in my classes and enjoyed seeing my friends, but as I got older I realized I really just hated being at home. My mom rarely attended school functions like award ceremonies and band concerts but when she did she usually came late and was wearing pj's. I almost never invited friends to my house as I was embarrassed of where we lived and even more so was embarrassed of my mom. Once I was old enough to spend the night with friends and got to see how they interacted with their mothers was when I truly realized the issues with my own mom. I always kind of thought that moms were just mean until I had friends with nice moms and quickly learned nice moms were normal. I also spent a lot of time with my grandparents growing up, which was mostly because my mom often needed them to babysit. Their house was always more fun and felt more loving and caring, so I naturally always wanted to spend more time there, but for a long time they were unaware of how awful things were at my mom and stepdad's house. They just assumed I wanted to be at their house because they had Wi-Fi and cable, which we did not.[3]

Dilek Shares the Daily Challenges with Her Overdrinking Father

My father was an overdrinker. We lost him in 2019. My mother has never ever tasted alcohol in her life, but me and her struggled with my father's drinking problems for years. I have seen my father drunk sleeping either on the stairs or the bathroom. He once had a very serious motorbike accident when I was only two years old. The doctors had said to my mom that he was about to die, and he was very drunk when they brought him to the hospital after the accident.

He was sober during the day because he was working at a tobacco factory as a security guard, but he was mostly drunk during the night. He had an extra job actually. He was a fisherman as well and after work, he used to come home, have something to eat, sleep for a couple of hours, and then go fishing. He used to stay at his small fishing boat till the morning. In the morning, he used to come home, sleep for a few hours, and go to work again. This was like a vicious cycle. We either did not see his face, saw him furious because of some reasons we never understood, or we saw him drunk shouting at everyone around him or throwing things at us without any reasons.

I remember a day. He was at home. He drank lots of things one after another. Then, he got drunk. And he rushed into the bathroom obviously to vomit. He did, and then fell asleep. On the ground! It was cold! I was very upset, and I remember crying almost till night. My mom was very angry and upset too. She did not let me wake him up and take him to his bed. He slept there until the morning, woke up and then went to work! This is my worst and the most heart-breaking memory! Worse than being beaten!

It was like having to be always alert and anxious because there was always a possibility of a fight at home. Home was far away from being a safe haven or a loving place for me. It was rather a place where I never felt relaxed, loved, cared for, and safe enough. It was an unstable and uncertain life where everything could happen at every moment.[4]

Georgianne's Experience
Their drinking affected everyday life as in not being able to have friends over or have any kind of parties. I was always worried I'd be embarrassed by their actions and if I was at school or somewhere other than home, I expected to get a phone call with bad news.[5]

Sarah's Experience
If she was home, she was locked in her room doing God knows what. Drinking, crying, smoking, screaming on the phone. It was horrible. I could never have friends over. I was ashamed constantly. Sometimes I would come home and every once in a while, she wouldn't be drinking. I would pray for a normal mother. I suffered socially, emotionally, physically, and mentally from her drinking. I would go to school with no sleep and come home to pure stress. She would say hurtful things to everyone in my family and I would always worry that she was dead when she passed out from all of her drinking.

I couldn't focus properly on school because I usually hadn't eaten anything. My mom didn't cook, and she spent all of our money on alcohol. I had no energy to fuel me properly. Because she kept me locked at home amidst her drinking, I didn't get to properly socialize with other children. I was so severely shy that they put me in the special ed department in school because I was scared to speak. I tested out very quickly when they learned I was just so nervous to raise my hand. It was hard to make friends because my clothes always smelled of smoke and I always had baggy hand-me-downs. If I did make a friend, I couldn't invite my friends over to the house because of the mess and her drinking. My dad forced my mom to get a job at the school as a lunchroom monitor. It was hard seeing her some days on the playground because I hadn't seen her in weeks. At home, she hid from me and spent all of her time drunk. At school I would see her, and she would act like nothing had happened. Everyone said my mom was so nice. It hurt because at

Figure 2.1 *Hurtful words are often said, painful memories are often created, and bad things usually happen when your parent overdrinks. Yelling can make you feel like it's directed toward you personally and might even scare you, and it is something that can take time for you to heal from.* (Illustration by Kate Haberer).

home she was the opposite. One day, I had no clean underwear to wear so I had to find a bathing suit bottom to wear instead. My mom caught glimpse of this on the playground one day when I bent over and proceeded to point, laugh and make fun of me amidst the other lunchroom monitors. I wanted to scream.

She was court ordered to attend AA [Alcoholics Anonymous] after several DUIs [driving under the influence] and run-ins with the law. To this day, she acts like she does not drink. Nothing has ever worked for her. We would write her letters, beg, cry, yell, anything for her to please stop. Nothing ever worked.[6]

Megan's Story
So, my father tried to make each day go as smoothly as possible. My mother and father argued when my mother was drinking but my father wisely stayed away from her when she was drunk. Nothing good came from interacting with her in that state. When she was sober, they argued sometimes but less often than you would expect. My father and mother loved each other very deeply and while her addiction caused so much pain and stress, my father made it work because he loved her so much. Sometimes I think about how life could have gone differently if my father had attended Al-Anon meetings. Fortunately, today it's much easier for people affected by addiction and their families to get the resources and help they need.[7]

Living and coping with a parent who overdrinks is challenging and life is quite different for teens compared to the experiences of their peers who don't have a parent who overdrinks. Sometimes families deal with the overdrinking behavior quietly and privately behind closed doors, while other families have to suffer from embarrassment and humiliation out in public.

Skeeter's Humiliating Restaurant Experience
It was my father's birthday one year and he booked a party of about twelve at a local restaurant. My boyfriend and I attended thinking

we were just going to a normal birthday dinner at a restaurant with some family members. We unfortunately had no clue what we were walking into.

We got to the restaurant on time, but when we arrived my father was already drunk. He apparently invited someone extra and the restaurant's biggest table was only big enough for twelve people not thirteen. The staff was trying to accommodate my father's new and last-minute reservation change, but it was already during dinner rush hour, so they made our party have to wait until after our reservation time to be seated. It wasn't the restaurant's fault, it was my father's, but due to his drunken state, he harassed the staff like it was their fault. He asked to see the manager and complained to where the manager even threw in some free appetizers in apology—something I felt was so wrong because the staff and restaurant didn't do anything wrong. By the time we were all seated, my father of course kept ordering more and more drinks. But with everything that came out for the rest of the night, between food and drinks, my father complained about everything. We tried speaking up to tell my dad that everything was fine to help alleviate the stress he was putting on the staff—in return for my father to say we were disrespecting him on his birthday. So it's like we all had to sit there and be quiet and let him be rude. We kept apologizing to the staff and we even left a very large collective tip at the end to offer our apologies for my father's behavior. The dinner was an awful experience—not because of the staff but because my father ruined what was supposed to be a fun night out of celebrating. We were embarrassed and humiliated as other guests at the restaurant were whispering and staring at us the whole time. I don't know why the restaurant didn't kick us out, or why we all didn't just get up and leave, but I wish they did, or we did. I apologized to my boyfriend all the way home because that wasn't fair for him to experience that.

That was the last time I ever ate at a restaurant with my father ever again. I refused every invitation since because that wasn't the first time he acted drunk and rude and belligerent at a restaurant- but that was my last time of dealing with his behavior at a restaurant.[8]

Figure 2.2 *Going out in public is supposed to be a fun and memorable experience with your parents. With an overdrinking parent, something as simple as going out to a restaurant together can become a stressful ordeal filled with embarrassment, regret, and loathing due to the scenes they cause.* (Illustration by Kate Haberer).

If you have one parent who overdrinks and one parent who is always sober, if you're too afraid to speak up to the overdrinking parent about your feelings, sometimes it can help to talk to the sober parent. If both parents overdrink, then a friend, neighbor, or outside family member might be a positive outlet for you to vent to and share your feelings with. It's always good to have someone in your corner that you can express your feelings freely and honestly with. Living with a parent who overdrinks is no picnic. It can be very emotionally draining and challenging. Don't feel like you have to go through this situation alone.

Veronica's Story

There are many [painful memories], but I would say the [worst were the] countless nights where I would wait up with panic attacks wondering when my father would return home while my head was swarming with the questions: Where is he, is he alive, dead? Will the police find him? Who is he with? That, or ending the school day with the news that my father is in jail. I remember some days where my family and I would all enjoy a nice day out and things would go sour because of his drinking when we returned.

[Daily life was] Chaotic. Frightening. Unpredictable, yet predictable. Most days were stressful, and I never knew what would happen next. When there would be a relief from the drinking, there was always a fear and an anxiety of when it would happen next, constant feelings of unsafety, and an negative aura day-to-day. There was an unnatural routine (which no child/teen should expect or get used to) to my daily life in the sense that I knew what to expect (most of the time) from my father when he would return home or when he would not; a very poisonous pattern. I would be very hypervigilant toward my father's behavior (and the environment in general) prior to his intoxication, during intoxication, and after. I would fight constantly, almost daily with my father, which caused me a lot of distress; I just wanted his attention, positive or negative. You never know which version of your parent you will get: Will you receive the good, the somewhat

nice, levelheaded parent who can get things done, or the negative, angry, and frightening parent that breeds chaos? It was also difficult to witness and feel the fear and anxiety that resulted from my parents' arguments and the general tension in the household that remained in the atmosphere of the home for some time, almost indefinitely. It was a lonely, anxiety inducing, terrifying time. My father's drinking was just something that had to be endured with no promise of it getting better. I did not realize how it would affect me until later on in my late teens and early adult years.[9]

CHAPTER 3

Dealing in Silence

How It Led to This

THE FIRST STEP TO IMPROVING A PROBLEM IS ACKNOWLEDGING the problem itself. If you are living with a parent who overdrinks, overdrinking is the problem. But if your parent doesn't acknowledge that they have an overdrinking problem, the problem won't improve—it will just stay the same or get worse. The people around the overdrinker can see that there's a problem, but unless the overdrinker acknowledges they have an overdrinking problem, then they will never see an issue with their behavior. If they don't acknowledge their behavior, then the people who are closest to them might be dealing with the overdrinking problem in silence. Sometimes those closest to the overdrinker are too embarrassed to admit to others that they are living with a parent who overdrinks. Often the fact that the parent denies they have an overdrinking problem causes those closest to them to deal with it in silence. If they openly talk about it, they are afraid of arguments that might arise, or it almost develops like some secret—although everyone around the overdrinker knows they have a drinking problem.

Skeeter's Dealing in Silence

My father started drinking before he was ten years old. He watched his father drink before him who watched his father drink before him. It's been a generational vicious cycle that doesn't seem to end. Everyone who knows my father knows he has an overdrinking problem, but over the years I've learned something—no one has ever confronted my father about his drinking problem to his face. People have mentioned it to me behind his back and have admitted he is a functioning over-drinker, but my father flat out denies he has a drinking problem. It's become this big elephant in the room at gatherings where everyone knows my father overdrinks, but my father won't admit it and no one will confront him about it. The couple of times I tried to talk to him about his drinking problem he became enraged with me and said I was disrespecting him because he's not an overdrinker like his father before him was. So him yelling at me when I tried to confront him about his problems and how his overdrinking makes me feel, has caused me to deal with it silently. He is like a bully and even one of his closest friends called him a narcissistic bully, behind his back of course, and I'm his daughter that he bullies when I'm just trying to tell him how I feel. What father bullies his daughter when she's just trying to share her feelings with her father? I'm trying to understand, offer help, and strengthen my relationship with my father. I even went to bartending school to try and see the other side of it, to see what was so great about alcohol to try and better understand my father. When he gets enraged with me it breaks my heart and makes our father–daughter relationship weaker. My mother already died when I was young, and I'm trying to salvage my relationship with my father, but the alcohol is winning. It's coming in between my father and I and we're running out of time to work this out. I'm trying to talk to him about my feelings because I don't want to suffer in silence anymore.

I have this daydream that one day my father will call me and tell me he stopped drinking and checked himself into rehab and then we could finally start a healing journey together. But each year that passes by, he's still drinking the same or more and he's getting older and starting to have health problems stemming from his drinking. I feel like I can't compete with the alcohol anymore and that my father already chose the bottle over me decades ago. I feel defeated like the bottle is more important and that he loves the bottle more than he will ever love me.[1]

Sarah's Story

I thought it was a secret and I did my best to hide it as a child but as I grew older, I learned that most people knew there was something very wrong with my family. The most heart broken I have ever felt in my life, was when I had been saving up all the money in my piggy bank to buy a kitten. I wanted a kitten because I had no friends. Since my mother suffered from mental health issues and was always drinking, she didn't properly socialize me and would not give me opportunities to play with other children. She was constantly drunk. Because of all this, I was instantly an outcast and had no friends. The piggy bank held all of my hope because if I could save up for a kitten, at least I wouldn't be so lonely. Maybe people would even want to be friends with me because I had a kitten, I remember thinking. One night, alone at home with my belligerently drunk mother, I discovered her on the bathroom floor breaking open my piggy bank with a hammer. She shattered it to the floor and was stealing my pennies, dollars, etcetera, to buy more alcohol. My heart quivered and I had never felt more alone in my life.[2]

Megan's Story

As I did everything I could think of doing to try to convince my mother to stop drinking, I worked hard to keep it a secret. My aunts and uncles and grandparents were aware of my mother's "drinking problem," but both families included generations of alcoholics, so they were raised to keep those problems a secret, too. Also, I do not think any of those family members, including my father, knew how much my mother's drinking was affecting me. I wish I'd been aware at the time that my mother's addiction to alcohol had absolutely nothing to do with me and that there nothing I could do to control it.

Figure 3.1 *Oftentimes your overdrinking parent is just focused on what they feel their needs or wants are. They aren't paying attention or realize that their decisions can hurt others around them, especially you, their teenage son or daughter.* (Illustration by Kate Haberer)

At school, it appeared I had a healthy homelife. I achieved good grades, always followed the teachers' directions, and never got into trouble. My teachers commented that I was lucky to have such wonderful parents. They were good people, but my mother's disease caused chaos and destructive behavior that deeply affected my sister and me. I had become very skilled at covering up what was happening at home.

When I was a teenager, I grew frustrated and angry that my mother continued to drink. As I realized she needed help to do that, I felt hurt she didn't love my sister and me enough to seek out and accept help. I felt she was choosing not to get help, and ultimately, choosing alcohol over her family. I avoided inviting any friends from school over to the house. The few times friends stopped by unexpectedly, my mother was drunk in the middle of the day, and I was humiliated. My best friend was the only non-family member who knew about my mother's drinking, but we rarely spoke of it because I did not want her to pity me. My father was the only parent involved in my sports and academics, so like in elementary school, my teachers and sports coaches believed I had an idyllic home environment.

Our neighbors, however, were aware of my mother's drinking. Most of them kept their distance from her. One neighbor reached out to try to help us a few times, but I was too ashamed to talk with her about it and too afraid my mother would be angry that I talked with her. I greatly regret not responding to that kind neighbor.[3]

FEELING ALONE

Sometimes it is comforting to know that there is someone else out there in the universe that understands what you are going through. It's a human element that connects us to one another. After all, we want to be connected, to feel loved, to feel understood, right? Well, what if none of your other friends have an overdrinking parent? Or any of your peers at school? Nor a neighbor or fellow churchgoer? You will want to be careful connecting with people you don't know in chat rooms, because just because someone says they are your age and have an overdrinking parent, doesn't mean that what they are saying via the internet is true. Sometimes, a safer way to feel a connection so you don't feel alone is to turn to societal figures. Many societal figures have a history of overdrinking parents that not many know about.

FAMOUS OVERDRINKING PARENTS

- Actress Jamie Lee Curtis: Known for her roles in movies such as the *Halloween* franchise, *True Lies*, and her children's book series,[4] her father struggled with alcohol.[5]
- Actor Ben Affleck has battled alcoholism, and his father and other family members struggled with alcohol as well.[6]
- Actress Carol Burnett had alcoholic parents and now is witnessing other family members struggling with it.[7]
- Actress Demi Moore struggled with alcoholism, and she relapsed when her daughter was just nine years old.[8]
- Actor Martin Sheen had a wake-up call from his alcoholism. He and his son Emilio have a strained relationship.[9]
- Actor Robin Williams: In 2006 Robin Williams was being treated for alcoholism. His daughter was a teenager at the time.[10]
- Nobel Prize Laureate Winner of 1936 Eugene O'Neill received the Nobel Prize in Literature. His father was an alcoholic. Addiction is a recurring theme in his works as his mother was also addicted to morphine.[11]
- Nobel Prize Laureate Winner of 1954 Ernest Hemingway, also a father, won the Nobel Prize in Literature and overdrank alcohol.[12]

Whatever your reason is for suffering, I hope after reading this you don't suffer in silence anymore. If your overdrinking parent is in denial, can you share your feelings with your sober parent? Another family member? Your best friend? A teacher? A neighbor? Your coach? Your school counselor? If you still don't have anyone you can share your feelings with, can you share your thoughts in a diary? Or a healthy coping outlet such as artwork or through music? Please don't think you have to continue suffering in silence. Suffering in silence means you're internalizing your feelings and bottling everything inside. That's not healthy for you and can have consequences for you in the future. You're never alone. Please don't suffer in silence anymore.

Veronica's Story

It was known by some people I am sure . . . the people who lived in our apartment. The friends that I had did not know. For me, how it felt inside, it was definitely something that I had to hide, and it made me feel different, flawed, and broken in comparison to others.[13]

Denial is an important component of the SUD (substance use disorder) family system. No one is supposed, or allowed, to know what is really going on. Denial has a debilitating effect on child development. The stress of keeping the family secret forces children to internalize their feelings and emotions and fosters a sense of helplessness.[14]

CHAPTER 4

Exposure to Abuse

FOR SOME OF YOU, OVERDRINKING AND BAD PARENTAL BEHAVIOR is not as far as this situation goes. Some of you, sadly, have been exposed to and a victim of different types of abuse. If this has been happening to you, please reach out to a trusted adult immediately so the abuse can be stopped. Look also in the resources section in the back of this book for important phone numbers and websites to help direct you to people who are safe and can help remove you from the abusive situation you might find yourself in. Abuse is never okay—physical, sexual, mental, emotional, or spiritual. Living with an overdrinking parent can already be subjecting you to mental, emotional, or psychological abuse, so adding additional types of abuse is just going to make things worse for you and further delay your healing.

SEXUAL ABUSE

MOVIE BREAK: *THE BUTTERFLY EFFECT*

In the 2004 movie *The Butterfly Effect*, the fictional characters Kayleigh (played by actress Amy Smart) and Tommy (played by actor William Lee Scott) are subjected, by

Tommy's dad (played by Eric Stoltz), to sexual abuse. He is often drunk when he abuses them. Throughout the movie, the audience sees the aftereffects of all the years of drunken sexual abuse the father gave the two children and how difficult their lives became as they grew up. They often dealt with the abuse silently, not knowing or understanding what was truly going on because, after all, children trust their parents. As they should be able to. It is not until years after they enter adulthood that they look back at their childhood and finally understand what really went on all those years. This is where Evan (played by Ashton Kutcher) tries to alter time to prevent the abuse from ever happening.[1]

Although I wish you could travel back in time like Evan did in the movie to change your parent's overdrinking behavior, and perhaps some painful memories, time travel unfortunately only exists in the movies. That means that these situations are real—you cannot erase what has happened, which is why it is important that you realize there is help out there for you, so you don't just have to accept what has been happening to you. It is not okay for anyone to ever abuse you. If this has been happening to you, although it might be scary, you need to tell someone what is going on. Please promise me that you will not keep this a secret. It will be forever incredibly damaging to you if you keep this a secret. The sooner you tell someone this has happened to you or has been happening to you, the sooner you can get help and the sooner it can be stopped and prevented from ever happening to you ever again. But, if you don't take the first step by alerting someone that this is indeed happening, how can anyone help you? There are counselors, national hotline numbers, teachers, coaches, church pastors, family members, friends, and more that you can tell. Again, abuse is not okay. If your overdrinking parent has been hurting you, sexually or otherwise, please tell someone right away so this can be stopped immediately. The longer it goes on, the more it can affect you mentally, psychologically, and physically.

MOVIE BREAK: *FORREST GUMP*

We see it again in the 1994 movie *Forrest Gump* when Jenny (played by actress Robin Wright) is sexually and physically abused by her father who is often drunk. There is a scene where Forrest (played by actor Tom Hanks) goes to visit Jenny, and she takes him away from her house as her drunken father is yelling at Jenny to come home. She prays in that moment to become a bird so she can fly far away. She wants to get away from her sexually and physically drunken abusive father, but being a child, she doesn't know how to. Forrest does not comprehend what is going on. Shortly after, her father is arrested and her prayers are answered, as she is sent to live with her grandmother. Yet, the mental, physical, and psychological damage was already done. Jenny had suffered so much abuse by that point, and she grows up to live a very destructive lifestyle as her way to cope with years of physical and sexual abuse. She didn't have to go down this road, however. She could have sought out help or enrolled in counseling sessions. She realizes that toward the end of the movie.[2]

Don't wait too long to get help. The sooner you reach out to a trusted adult for help the sooner you can help yourself heal from the awful events that may have happened to you. If you are or have been getting physically or sexually abused by your overdrinking parent, please tell someone immediately. It is not okay. If you don't trust any of the adults around you, then please reach out to any of the national hotline numbers listed in the resources section in the back of this book. You can even contact me directly, and I will help point you in the right direction for some help.

PHYSICAL ABUSE

MOVIE BREAK: *THE SHACK*

In the 2017 movie *The Shack*, Mack (played by actor Sam Worthington) is a young boy with an overdrinking father who beats him and his mother up regularly. He has painful memories later as an adult looking back at his difficult childhood. Papa (played by actress Octavia Spencer) later lets Mack see his father who used to abuse him to where they even have a moment of forgiveness. Papa points out that Mack's dad had an abusive and alcoholic father before him, and this shows how it has been a terrible cycle throughout generations. Papa gives Mack this moment as he is navigating another tragic difficult life situation that leads him to visit a mysterious shack as part of his healing journey.[3]

MOVIE BREAK: *I CAN ONLY IMAGINE*

In the 2018 movie *I Can Only Imagine*, Bart (played by actor John Michael Finley) lives with his alcoholic and abusive father, Arthur (played by actor Dennis Quaid). Arthur had suffered an injury that has changed him into an abusive alcoholic. Bart spends most of his childhood living in fear for himself and his mother. His mother leaves him to live with his father. Arthur is terrible to Bart, often crushing his dreams, throwing his creative inventions away, yelling at him, and throwing plates at him. He is awfully abusive to Bart. One day, Bart has had enough, and he leaves. Music is his coping mechanism and so he leaves to pursue his dream of becoming a singer. He doesn't talk to his father for years until he returned to a changed father. Arthur has left his alcoholic and abusive past behind him and turned to God. He is a changed man. There is even a little time left for Bart and Arthur to heal their past and reconcile when Bart learns his father is dying.[4]

Dilek's Story

Almost everyone knew it because, when he was drunk, there was always chaos or a fight at home and, unfortunately, he used to beat me or my mother a lot because of tiny reasons. So, my mom's family used to learn what happened at our home right away.[5]

Sometimes you might not be directly involved with the physical or sexual abuse, but you witness it happening before your very eyes to another household family member. Sometimes in ways you become indirectly involved and get brought into the fight, or feel like you suddenly have to fight back. These are not fun scenarios to be in. Someone will always get hurt in the end—whether physically or emotionally, mentally, or psychologically.

Georgianne's Story

There were so many bad days it's hard to pick the worst one. Perhaps the worst was when my mother ended up with a broken nose because when I saw that, I went after my stepfather with a baseball bat and my older brother tried to get in a fight with him and ended up breaking a large window in the business. My mother was very physically, mentally, and verbally abusive to me but not to my other siblings.[6]

Skeeter's Story

I remember I was in my room doing my homework after school one day. I heard some loud noises coming from the kitchen. I went to investigate. When I got closer to the kitchen, I heard my father and brother arguing really loudly and like they were chasing each other in the kitchen. My mother just passed away the year before and things were just always tense. My father was drinking a little more and he and my brother were just always clashing. When I turned the corner to the kitchen, I remember starting to shake because I was so scared. I saw my father gripping my brother's T-shirt neckline and they were in each other's faces screaming at each other. Both had cuts on their face and neck as if they were trying to grab and fight each other. I was barely ten years old, and their aggressive confrontation was terrifying me. I didn't know what to do. I tried to tell them both to stop but it's like they were in a trance I couldn't get them out of. The only thing I could think of was I ran out the door and tried to get one of the neighbors. I told them what was going on and they headed over to try and help stop the fight. Looking back now I don't know if that was the best idea, but as a kid that was the only one I had. By the time the neighbor showed up, they had stopped fighting. My brother angrily went to his room and slammed the door. My father got in his car and drove off. The neighbor asked if I was okay alone after that and I said yes. I was pretty shaken up. I felt like after my mom died our family was just falling apart. I went back to my room and locked my door. I went to bed early that night, still scared that they would start fighting again. I don't think my dad came home until the next afternoon, and my brother didn't come out of his room until the next morning.

The worst fight while my dad was drunk that I remember is he and my mother, who was sick and dying, were arguing in the living room together. My brother and I heard the commotion and went toward the living room. When we got there, my dad got so angry at my mom that he physically pushed her, right in front of us. She fell over and tripped over the couch ottoman. I was so mad at my dad for hurting my mother while he was drunk that night. He tried apologizing to all of us shortly after, but that was the night my mother took my brother and I away from home and we stayed at a hotel for the next two days. The fact that he pushed my very sick mother in his drunken state—it's an image I can't unsee, although I wish I could.[7]

Sarah's Story
My mom would say the most heinous things while drunk. She would strip naked, wear pearls around her neck after chugging several packs of Miller Light. She would come out in the living room and scream at my father. She would scream that he was probably cheating on her and throw lamps at him. She would attempt to hit him and stumble over herself. I didn't understand any of this as a child, but it made me feel so hurt. She would scream at me that I was a selfish brat or that I had mental problems. As a child, she would leave me home alone without food for hours, sometimes days. She would force me into the car while she was incredibly drunk, so that she could drive up to the local drug drugstore to buy more beer. I was up for hours late at night, listening to her scream, drunk-call people, cry, etcetera. It was horrible.[8]

Veronica's Story
Occasionally [there was] physical [abuse], but only when I engaged in confrontation.[9]

PSYCHOLOGICAL ABUSE
Another type of abuse that is common for teenagers and young adults living with an overdrinking parent is psychological abuse. What is psychological abuse? Psychological abuse is the deliberate use of words used with the intent to

Figure 4.1 *No teenager wants to hear their parents fighting. Overdrinking parents seem to have yelling come with the territory. However, when the yelling turns to physical fights between your parents, it is an unhealthy and dangerous situation for everyone in the house.* (Illustration by Kate Haberer).

hurt, manipulate, frighten, confuse, or influence someone else. So, take a step back and think about it for a second. Has your overdrinking parent ever denied that something happened?—"I didn't make a scene at the restaurant; you are making up stories," or, "I never said that, you must have heard that wrong"—when you specifically remember them causing that scene at the restaurant or saying something. In most cases you even have the proof that you were right and they were wrong. That was your overdrinking parent trying to gaslight you. They might have tried to gaslight you to alleviate their guilty conscience, or to erase the transgression they know they have in their heart. Has your overdrinking parent ever told you while they are drunk things like "you will never amount to anything," "no one will love you," "no one will believe you?" The list goes on and on of all of the little things they can say to try to mess with your personal state of mind. Their words may seem little, but the effect they can have on your psychological health and well-being make them large and powerful and can affect you for years to come without you even realizing it.

You are still young, and if you are less than twenty-five years old and reading this, your brain is technically not all the way developed yet. So any experience you have, anything said to you or done to you, is still impacting your brain development. This is why it is so important for you to reach out to a trusted and safe adult that can help you—a counselor, a teacher, a coach, a relative, and so on—so you can stop the abuse from happening and stop it from impacting your brain as it develops. What happens to you when you are young carries on into your adulthood. The more negative experiences you have while growing up, the more struggles you might have as a result of them later.

What is the ACEs Quiz? ACE stands for *adverse childhood experiences*, and the summary behind the test is the more adverse childhood experiences you have, the more complicated your life might be as an adult because you will have to recover from all that you dealt with. The quiz asks you a series of questions pertaining to what you were exposed to while growing up. Some questions include: Did you have a parent addicted to alcohol or drugs while growing up? Did you witness a parent being abused? Were you a victim of physical, sexual, or verbal abuse? The more questions you answer yes to equals your total ACE score at the end. If you want to see where you are at, take the ACEs quiz at https://americanspcc.org/take-the-aces-quiz/ and you will know if you are on the high or low end.[10]

It is better to have as few negative life events as possible, as some things will always happen along the way to anyone while growing up—maybe being exposed to bullying at school or falling off a bike and suffering an injury—but psychological abuse by your overdrinking parent, because they are your parent and one of the closest life bonds you will form throughout your entire lifetime, can have profound effects on your overall psychological well-being. The sooner the abuse is recognized, the sooner steps can be taken to stop it. Remember that the rule of thumb is it will take half the time you experienced something negative for you to properly move forward in a healthy healing way. In other words, if your parent has been psychologically abusing you for the last ten years, you are looking at roughly five years to heal and move forward in a healthier direction—but that is only if the abuse stops, or you are no longer living under the same roof as the overdrinking, psychologically abusive parent. It is hard to heal while the abuse is still occurring.

Verbal Abuse

When living in a household where you have one or two over-drinking parents, yelling typically comes with the territory. Whether you are the one getting yelled at, your siblings are getting yelled at, or your two overdrinking parents or one overdrinking parent and one sober parent are yelling at each other. Some other bystanders might get involved in the yelling as well, let's say a neighbor yells at your overdrinking parent for yelling so loudly, or if a family friend or other relative is present when the overdrinker is having a drunken episode, they can get involved with the yelling too.

Just a guess, but you probably aren't a fan of the yelling. Who wants to get yelled at or be near where people are yelling? It stresses you out whether you are getting yelled at. It makes people's hearts race. It makes everyone walk on eggshells around the person who is yelling—no one wants to spend time with this person. Yelling makes people feel bad inside and uncomfortable. It can also do long-term damage emotionally and psychologically. People naturally want to be happy. I don't know anyone who purposely wants to be unhappy. Yelling isn't any fun. Even the person yelling can feel tremendous guilt afterward because they feel bad for yelling or hurting others. In this case, your overdrinking parent or parents could be battling feeling guilty after having yelled at you, your sibling, or their spouse—if they remember what they did while they were overdrinking, that is.

Constant yelling, like daily yelling, can lead to you being subjected to verbal abuse. It's not just the physical part of your overdrinking parent yelling in general, but the words they are yelling can deeply affect you as well. Do they put you down when they yell? Call you names? Say hurtful things to other family members right in front of you? According to Merriam-Webster, verbal abuse is harsh and insulting language directed at a person. Take a step back and think for a second. Does your overdrinking parent yell at you when they are drunk? When they are sober? Do they yell at you or other family members in your household? Have they yelled things at you or others that are mean and hurtful? Have their words hurt you before? If so, you may have been getting verbally abused by your overdrinking parent without even knowing it.

If you have been victimized by your overdrinking parent's verbal abuse, reach out to a trusted adult for help. No one deserves to be abused in any way, and if your overdrinking parent is doing that to you, it needs to stop. We can't just excuse them for their behavior saying that it's okay for an overdrinking parent to constantly verbally abuse their child because they cannot help that their drunkenness affects their brain. Where is the line drawn? What about how you have the right to not have an overdrinking verbally abusive parent? There has to be a line drawn somewhere. Reach out to your sober parent or trusted relative, school counselor, employee assistance program at your job, outside counselor, priest, or coach for help so the verbal abuse can stop. I hope you have someone you can trust in your life to be in a safe place to express yourself, as some teens and young adults will just bottle everything inside and avoid being home to avoid their overdrinking parent. That is not a fair way for you to live, always dodging your overdrinking parent or avoiding your house because you know they will be there. You have a right to a safe home that provides your basic needs, and if your overdrinking parent's behavior is blocking that, then that is not right, and you need some help and guidance to improve the situation. Don't keep it to yourself. Explore options with a trusted adult in your life so you can break free from the verbally abusive, overdrinking parent. Dealing with an overdrinking parent is difficult enough—dealing with one or two verbally abusive, overdrinking parents is too much to handle at such a young age.

Veronica's Story
I do not recall being hit with anything, but there was verbal and emotional abuse.[11]

Approximately 53 percent of Americans have one or more close relatives who have an alcohol dependency problem. In addition, 43 percent of American adults have been exposed to the problem of alcoholism in the family, either as something they grew up with or something they experienced with a spouse or a partner.[12]

The Science and Research behind Overdrinking Behavior

IF YOU ARE NOT ABLE TO GET THROUGH TO HOW YOU ARE TRULY feeling with your overdrinking parent, and your sober parent is far too stressed out to have in-depth conversations about your overdrinking parent, perhaps learning about what happens to a person's brain and body can help you figure out part of what is really going on. You may not know why your parent drinks, but here is some science to show you the effects of overdrinking on the brain and the body. This doesn't justify why your parent says mean things to you when they overdrink, but learning about what alcohol does to the brain can help you better understand the drunk parent versus sober parent scenario better. If your overdrinking parent's physical health has changed, now you can see what overdrinking does to a person's body. Everyone's health is different, and alcohol and overdrinking can affect individuals differently, but here is some science and research to let you better interpret the overall situation.

Understanding Blood Alcohol Concentration and the Consequences

According to the National Institute on Alcohol Abuse and Alcoholism, as you drink, you increase your blood alcohol concentration (BAC), which is the amount of alcohol present in your bloodstream. The higher your BAC, the more impaired you become by alcohol's effects. The consequences of drinking too much alcohol include: reduced inhibitions, slurred speech, motor impairment, confusion, memory problems, concentration problems, coma, breathing problems, and even death.[1] So if you have ever witnessed your parent slurring their speech, struggling to breathe, or struggling with their memory after they overdrank, chances are their BAC was high at the time and they were facing the consequences. Think back to an episode of your parent overdrinking. If you remember any of these aftereffects, chances are your parent drank too much and their body was reacting to having too much alcohol in their bloodstream.

Alcohol Use Disorder

Alcohol use disorder (AUD) is a medical condition that is also considered a brain disorder. It involves having an impaired ability to stop or control alcohol use despite adverse social, occupational, or health consequences. Risk factors include family history, genetics, drinking at an early age, trauma, and mental health conditions. Although cases can range from mild to severe, there is good news for those suffering from AUD. Treatment, counseling, medication, and behavior therapies can help with recovery.[2] If your overdrinking parent is suffering from AUD, they can get the help they need. Their doctor can help guide them down a path to recovery. However, they have to want to stop drinking. No one can make them seek out help. No matter how hard you try to plead and beg with them, your overdrinking parent has to make that choice and take that positive step. You cannot force them to do it. There is help out there—it's just a question of whether your overdrinking parent wants to admit they have a problem and take the next steps to rehabilitate themselves, recover, and avoid relapses.

What Happens to the Brain When There Is Too Much Alcohol Consumed

When your parent overdrinks, the alcohol they consume creates challenges and problems for their brain to properly function in a healthy way. They suddenly can't control their balance, they have poor judgment, struggle with their memory, and slur their speech. Long-term heavy drinking can actually shrink their brain's neurons (nerve cells that are needed to communicate with their brain).[3] Has your parent ever blacked out on you after a period of overdrinking? Fell over after they lost their balance from overdrinking and injured themselves? When they came home from the bar, did their clothes, skin, and breath reek of alcohol? Did you hear them throwing up in the bathroom? Or find them passed out on the floor? Overdrinking causes all sorts of problems that can lead to even bigger problems, physically and mentally, as overdrinking affects the part of the brain needed to function with everyday skills.

Long-Term Physical Consequences of Your Parent Overdrinking

The longer your parent overdrinks, the more they increase their risk for a variety of health problems. This is not to scare you but to help educate you on possible warning signs that their health may be a direct result of their overdrinking. They are at risk for the following, some you may see signs of already:

- High blood pressure, heart disease, stroke, liver disease, and digestive problems
- Cancer of the breast, mouth, throat, esophagus, voice box, liver, colon, and rectum

- Weakening of the immune system, increasing the chances of getting sick
- Learning and memory problems, including dementia
- Mental health problems, including depression and anxiety
- Social problems, including family problems, job-related problems, and unemployment
- Alcohol use disorders or alcohol dependence[4]

Dilek's Story

[My overdrinking father] died of several complications and, yes, constant drinking caused some of them. He had diabetes, kidney failure, heart problems, and many more at a very young age.[5]

Overdrinking can affect major organ systems of the body and can deeply affect the health of a person's brain. It is not something to take lightly as the consequences can sadly be permanent if not addressed. There are steps your parent can take to reverse some of the damage they have done, the sooner the better, but, again, only they can make that choice. It is hard to watch your loved one head toward a brick wall that you know will keep knocking them down over and over. It is hard and even painful to just sit back and watch, to feel you can't do anything to stop it from happening. You love your overdrinking parent, but it is hard to try and navigate an overdrinking parent situation.

JODY LAMB'S EXPERT OPINION

Jody Lamb, an author—whose work was celebrated by the Betty Ford Center—speaker, and advocate for children of overdrinking parents, shares her expert insight when it comes to teenagers understanding what alcohol does to their overdrinking parent's brains:

"But if they really loved me, they wouldn't drink." Ever have that thought? People who have a parent who overdrinks often feel their parent is choosing alcohol over them. But the reality is overdrinking is usually a case of alcohol dependence, which is a medical disorder. The fact is people who overdrink lose their ability to control their drinking because their bodies become so dependent on it. The body becomes physically and emotionally dependent on alcohol to function properly and affects the brain. This happens over time as the person consumes more and more alcohol. Alcohol greatly affects how the person thinks and behaves because it affects the brain. Alcohol use disorders can often go undetected by most people who know the person because of how drinking is embedded in our society as a social activity.

The only way to stop drinking once you are dependent upon it is to get professional help to do so. Luckily, there are many programs and support groups to help people who want to stop drinking to overcome their alcohol use disorder. Some people take a very long time before they reach the point where they admit they have lost control over their drinking and want to overcome it. Sadly, some people never reach that point. Some are successful in overcoming their alcohol use disorder and some are not. What never changes is the fact that no one other than the person who uses alcohol can control their drinking. You cannot cause someone to overdrink and you cannot make someone stop drinking or drink less. What you can do is recognize that your parent's illness is theirs to get help for. Your parent's drinking has nothing to do with you, even if they tell you otherwise. Growing up, I experienced heartbreak every time my mother broke her promise to never drink again. I believed that she chose alcohol over me, and that meant she did not love me enough to stop. I thought it was my duty as her daughter to "fix" her. When I became an adult, I read about overdrinking and realized my mother has a substance use disorder and her body is dependent on alcohol to function.

Though my mother wanted to stop drinking, she could not unless she accepted professional help to do it and she was not ready to do that. Despite what little-kid-me believed, my mother loved me deeply, but was ill.

Focus on taking good care of yourself.[6]

CHAPTER 6

Teenagers Become the
Responsible Caretakers

PARENTS ARE SUPPOSED TO TAKE CARE OF THEIR CHILDREN.
NOT only is it a legal responsibility but also a moral one. Children
are not supposed to take care of their parents. It's been this way
for generations. Parents take care of their children. However, you
might notice that your overdrinking parent might have turned the
tables on you and instead of them taking care of you (what they
are supposed to be doing), you are suddenly taking care of them.
Just take a step back and ask yourself if you're not sure if the tables
have turned. Each night is your overdrinking parent making you
dinner or are you making them dinner? Is your overdrinking parent driving you to school or are you driving to pick them up from
the bar? Does your overdrinking parent help put you to bed when
you fall asleep at the kitchen table while doing your homework,
or are you putting your overdrinking parent to bed because you
found them passed out drunk on the living room couch again?
Sometimes it's hard to grasp the situation you are really in until
you take a step back and assess and analyze what's really going on.
Again, your overdrinking parent is supposed to take care of you,
their child. It's not supposed to be the other way around. You are
not supposed to be taking care of your overdrinking parent—but

for some of you, now you might realize your roles have changed with your overdrinking parent. Instead of them being the responsible one, somehow now you're more responsible than your overdrinking parent. That's a problem. That's not normal. That isn't right. Again, if you suddenly find yourself in this type of situation, you can try talking to your overdrinking parent when they're sober. If that is not possible, you can try talking to your sober parent, if that's an option, to help improve the situation at home. If the situation doesn't improve, that is when you need to reach out to your healthy positive support system so you can vent, whether it's to the Al-Anon support group you joined, to your coach or school counselor, or to your friend or relative. A non-overdrinking parent or someone close to you will really recognize that you becoming the caretaker is wrong on so many levels and will change it immediately. An overdrinking parent will not think they are forcing you into a caretaker role.

DEPENDENCY

Another side effect or negative factor that can come with living with an overdrinking parent is how dependent they can become on people around them. When your overdrinking parent is sober, they can thrive on their independence and even teach you life lessons on the importance of being independent. But when they become drunk or hungover the next day, suddenly your usually independent overdrinking parent is now super dependent. Dependent on needing to have someone pick them up from the bar or take them to pick up the car they left at the bar when they were too drunk to drive home. Dependent because they can't remember details from the days before and after they drank too much, or they forget to get groceries so someone else needs to do it, or they are too disoriented to cook the family dinner so someone else has to. The list goes on and on. We learned that alcohol affects the brain negatively and the more the parent drinks and the higher their BAC, or blood alcohol concentration, increases, the more their healthy brain functioning skills decrease. They can slur their speech, have memory loss, get super tired, smell of booze, be forgetful, lose their balance, say terrible things, and more. The more your parent drinks and overdrinks, the harder life gets for the people around them. The overdrinking parent's health suffers, but overdrinking doesn't just affect the overdrinker—it affects everyone in their life, especially those living in the same household. "The brain actually changes with addiction, and it takes a good deal of work to get it back to its normal state. The more drugs or alcohol you've taken, the more disruptive it is to the brain."[1]

TAKING CARE OF OTHER SIBLINGS
Ava's Story
I often was responsible for my siblings and took care of changing their diapers and dressing them and making them food. As for school, I often was responsible for getting myself up and making sure to catch the bus and if I missed the bus I was in huge trouble.[2]

Georgianne's Story
Since I was the oldest daughter, I had more responsibilities with taking care of my younger siblings and had been called home several times to either try to stop the fighting or look for the younger ones because they would run and hide across the highway or in a field. [My mother and stepfather] never blamed me or my siblings for their drinking problems. I carried the burden of feeling responsible for taking care of my mother and my siblings all of my life, which means I didn't have a good life and made bad choices myself. Not alcohol or drugs though, that was doled out among my siblings.[3]

Megan's Story
My mother's substance use disorder had a profound impact on my childhood. I had to become a mini adult at a very young age. I became hypervigilant, responsible for things that should have been taken care of by my parents.[4]

Skeeter's Story

In my early twenties, my dad caught wind that I was making good money right out of college. Several series of events occurred that have financially impacted me to this day. To all you readers, please learn from my mistakes. Yes, we love our parents and want to do anything to help them. But please remember that their overdrinking can cloud even our judgment. My judgment was severely clouded, and years later I am still paying for that mistake.

My father was out of work and hurting for money. He just went through his third divorce after the death of my mother. He hardly had any food in his house, he fell into a depression, wasn't sleeping, his electricity kept getting shut off. I have never seen my father so depressed and just defeated. I was making good money in my early twenties with little bills and little responsibilities, so I decided to help my father. Noble cause, yes, but not when your father overdrinks. I rallied and talked to all of my family members and father's closest friends and told them that due to his divorce he was struggling mentally and emotion-ally and now financially. My father has a good heart and is a good man when he is sober. So everyone started throwing money at my dad. He was able to catch up on bills, buy his medicine, turn his electricity back on, buy food. It was amazing. I helped him too. I had credit cards with high limits so I started charging everything on my cards knowing that I could pay my credit card bills in full at the end of the month. I also took out a loan in my name to help my father secure his own place. I even tried to buy a house and was going to let my dad live with me. As the months went by and my father was digging his way out, I started noticing that he was going to the bar a lot more. I looked at his bills and he was still behind. Turns out, he used the money we were all giving to him to buy wants instead of catching up on his needs. I found out he was using the money to go the bars and he was buying patrons rounds. He was also back to going to expensive steak house type restaurants.

The loan I took out capitalized with interest and I have been strug-gling to pay it ever since. I cannot get rid of the bill. I have been in col-lections over the years several times because at this point I cannot even afford to make the minimum payments. My credit cards that I racked up for him capitalized with high interest rates. My job cut my hours due to the economy, so suddenly I couldn't afford the payments and had to file bankruptcy. I was just trying to help my father, but all the help and money I personally gave him and the help and money everyone else gave him just went to the bar. And I paid the price for that.

Parents shouldn't be taking money from their children. Parents are supposed to take care of, raise, and provide for their children. Not the other way around. My dad never really owned up to that or apologized. I know that if my dad was a sober dad instead of an overdrinking one, that he never would have taken advantage of his daughter like that. He hindered my future. But it was my fault because I inadvertently let him.[5]

JODY LAMB'S EXPERT OPINION ON TEENAGERS ASSUMING THE CARETAKER ROLE

Jody Lamb, author, speaker, and advocate for children of overdrinking parents, shares her expert insight when it comes to teenagers becoming caretakers and the responsible ones when they have parents who overdrink:

From organizing cupboards to reminding a parent to pay the electricity bill, it is common for someone with a parent who overdrinks to take on adult responsibilities at a young age. It's no wonder this happens. Overdrinking can cause a parent to forget or be unable to take care of their children and other adult responsibilities. Some kids start taking on these responsibilities themselves, thinking, "Well, somebody has to do it." If you're the oldest kid in your family, this may particularly ring true for you.

Taking on adult responsibilities can quickly become a habit for kids. After a while, it may feel like it is your job to take care of these tasks for your parent, even though it is not. It is totally normal to have this feeling. Some may even prefer to take care of the responsibilities for their parent because they are craving predictability and order in the household. If you cannot rely on your parent to fulfill their responsibilities because of their overdrinking, you may find it easier to do yourself. It may give you a sense of control over a few aspects of your life, while the rest of your life feels very out of control.

Overdrinking causes some parents to behave strangely and erratically—warm and calm one moment, cold and dismissive or abusive just a while later. Kids of people who overdrink become skilled at covering up for their parent's mistakes. You may not fully know what normal behavior for a parent is if your parent is often drinking, but by now, you probably know well what parents are supposed to do and not do. You may feel like you're always picking up all the messes—figuratively and literally— that come from your parent's overdrinking.

It is common for kids with parents who overdrink to become so obsessed with their parent's drinking that they no longer have their own lives.

Through this process of taking on many parental and adult responsibilities, you may even start to feel that your parent has become the child to be looked after and you have become the parent. This is what I call the "parent-kid role switcharoo" that comes from overdrinking and other challenges that prevent a parent from fulfilling their job responsibilities. For me, getting my mother to stop drinking became my life's quest so that my mother and our whole family could live happily ever after. At a young age, I became much more like a mother to my mother than I was a child.

If this sounds familiar to you, it's time to pause and recognize what is your job and what is not your job. Your only job in life is to take good care of yourself. That's it. It is not your job to take care of your parents or your siblings. It is not your job to act like an adult when you are not yet an adult. This can be hard to accept, especially if you have siblings, and you have been watching out for everyone since you were young. But it is very important to recognize this now so you can return to your role as the child, not the parent.

Being a parent to your parent can deeply harm your parent. If everything in your parent's life is functioning (at least on the surface), they may not have the drive or motivation to get help. When people in the overdrinking person's life take care of everything, they are enabling the person to keep overdrinking because there are never any life-changing circumstances that result from it. By enabling your parent to overdrink by taking care of many of their parent or adult responsibilities, you may be unknowingly preventing your parent from recognizing that their drinking is excessive and that they need help to overcome their alcohol dependence. You could be making it easier for them to keep things exactly as they are when what they really need is to realize they want help to stop overdrinking.[6]

What Is Enabling?

ACCORDING TO MERRIAM-WEBSTER, THE DEFINITION OF AN enabler is one who enables (makes it possible for) another to persist in self-destructive behavior (such as substance abuse) by providing excuses or by making it possible to avoid the consequences of such behavior. The person may not realize or even understand that they are supporting the bad behavior and may be doing so inadvertently.

When it comes to your overdrinking parent, you may have accidentally enabled them as well. It's hard not to because they are your parent, but enabling your overdrinking parent won't really help them in the long run. If you are wondering if you have ever enabled your overdrinking parent, ask yourself a few questions. Have you ever lied to cover up for your parent's overdrinking behavior? Does your overdrinking parent rely on you for car rides home from bars each time they get drunk? Do you choose restaurants that serve alcohol because you know your parent likes to drink (even though you know it will cause them to overdrink or encourage bad behavior)? This is a tricky situation with a difficult line that gets crossed, because on one hand, they are your parent and you want to please them—but on the other hand, their unhealthy decisions to overdrink are getting you caught in the middle.

MOVIE BREAK: *SAVING MR. BANKS*

In the 2013 movie *Saving Mr. Banks*, little Ginty (played by actress Annie Rose Buckley) inadvertently becomes her overdrinking father's enabler. She's so young and innocent that she does not realize that she's enabling her father (played by actor Colin Farrell). She has such a close relationship with him and although she knows he has a drinking problem, Ginty adores him and would do anything and everything he asks of her—even if he asks her to find a bottle of booze from a forbidden hiding place even while he's coughing and sick from drinking too much alcohol. Ginty would do anything her father asks of her, but she inadvertently is enabling her father. Ginty's mother (played by actress Ruth Wilson) learns that Ginty had been sneaking her father additional alcohol per his request and gets very mad with her daughter because she knows she is enabling him, almost like she's supporting her father's bad drinking habit. It makes her feel conflicted between the father she loves who overdrinks and the sober mother who is trying to get her to stop fueling the fire.[1]

Sometimes we manifest ourselves and our real-life experiences into various art forms and coping outlets. Actor Colin Farrell not only played Ginty's father in the movie *Saving Mr. Banks* but he also starred in a few other movies that show a parent struggling with overdrinking. Colin, who has struggled with overdrinking in real life and is a father himself, also starred in *Crazy Heart* and *Ondine*, which both feature overdrinking behavior.[2]

Georgianne's Story of Enabling

As a child or teen, you don't think about the word "enable." You don't even know what that is. You do as you're told by your parent even though it might be hard or you don't understand. You might think about how you can get out of what they're asking you to do or expect you to do because it may be scary or stressful, but it seems useless. You just do as you're told and, in some cases if you don't, then you face the consequences. Did I enable my mother? Of course. I helped her sneak her alcohol into the house and hide it from her spouse. And I always had to have one opened in another room for her to drink without her husband knowing whenever she signaled me to do it. In my case, it was a long time ago and there were not the resources there are now. I sincerely hope it is better for teens now in this day and age and would definitely encourage them to seek help [if they are getting caught in an enabling type of situation].[3]

Sometimes people enable on purpose while others accidentally do it, not realizing that they are even enabling to begin with. For example, your overdrinking parent most likely has some go-to buddies that overdrink like they do. Even though they all most likely know they overdrink, they can enable each other to drink more by inviting each other back to the bar over and over again. Other family members might not realize they are enabling when the overdrinking parent constantly asks for a ride home from the bar and a family member always picks them up. This is another tricky situation as having a parent who overdrinks get behind the wheel is irresponsible and can cause harm to them or someone else on the road who is innocent. But, constantly picking them up is basically saying that you are okay that they are constantly overdrinking and at the bar, and they can just call you and they know you will pick them up, almost like you are supporting their bad behavior. Skeeter, a participant for this book, shares:

My overdrinking father started having health problems that kept landing him in and out of the hospital that stemmed from his overdrinking. When he would have to stay in the hospital for sometimes a few days or even weeks, his drinking buddies would actually sneak in alcohol to him in the hospital room. I didn't hear about this until years later, but had I heard that was going on, I would have warned the nurses because him drinking alcohol in the hospital could have interfered with the medicine they were giving my father to try and get him out of the hospital.[4]

So again, it is a very tricky situation because on the one hand it's good that your overdrinking parent is calling for a ride home from the bar because that means they aren't getting behind the wheel drunk themselves. But, if this is a regular routine, then the overdrinking parent knows they can go to the bar and someone will pick them up. This is just creating a further toxic habitual routine that's not good either. There has to be some sort of boundary set where the overdrinking parent needs to be responsible while drinking and making decisions—but how can you expect them to be responsible when they're inebriated?

Skeeter's Story of Accidental Enabling

My father had this routine where pretty much every night at around 5 p.m., he would visit a bar. He always knew that he could drink as much as he liked and that he could call me when he was all done, no matter how late it was, and I'd drop what I was doing and pick him up. Now I feel so much guilt that I enabled him. Maybe he would have drank less had he not had a reliable ride home after getting drunk at the bar—and then I feel like I was responsible for his overdrinking behavior to continue as long as it did.

One night I got brave. I was sick and tired of having my life interrupted to enable my father or to constantly cater to his overdrinking behavior issues. I was exhausted from work one night. I was a college student full-time, I worked full-time, and I had pretty much another full-time job dealing with my overdrinking father. I just needed a break one night and didn't feel like playing my overdrinking father's pick-me-up-from-the-bar game. He asked me to come get him and for the first time ever, I actually said "no." He had never heard me say "no" before. To a sober person, this would have been okay, and they would have found a ride from someone else. To my overdrinking father, "no" became an instant trigger of rage. He completely went off on me. I was tired of being his enabler. He ended up walking home that night, which was about a two-mile walk. He was livid with me. I stupidly thought maybe the two-mile walk home would help him think about his life choices and maybe would give him a wake-up call to change his life around. Well, it didn't. It just caused a drunken fight that I was never going to win when he got home.[5]

Enabling and dealing with your overdrinking parent is hard. You want to help your overdrinking parent with whatever they ask of you because, simply put, they are your parent. There is a forever bond there. You feel bad standing up to them, but then you feel bad enabling them too and giving them what they want. Then you start to feel guilty because that is who raised you, and then you feel like you are being disrespectful. However, relationships are not one-sided—there are two people involved here. Yes, you should respect your parents, but shouldn't they respect you too?

A teenager of an overdrinking parent surely has an internal memory book of the painful memories that drinking behavior has caused over the years. While you don't want to focus on the pain and the bad memories, especially when you embark on your healing journey, some are too fresh to delete just yet. Reading stories of situations that happened to others also experiencing overdrinking parents can help you feel less alone in your journey. You might also be able to gauge your overdrinking parent situation to that of your fellow peers.

Enabling might not always be obvious. It is a hard situation to be in. You are too young to be forced in this type of situation to begin with.

CHAPTER 8

Sober Parent versus Drunk Parent

IF YOU HAVE ONE PARENT WHO OVERDRINKS AND ONE PARENT who is sober, perhaps you can share your feelings with your sober parent if you feel like you cannot connect with the overdrinker. Some of you, however, might have both parents who overdrink, which is incredibly challenging, and you'll have to try and find some outside support. Either situation is tricky and will come with its own challenges. Getting parented by your sober parent will be different than getting parented by your drunk parent. The sober parent might not always be 100 percent available to you as well, however, because they could be dealing with the added stress of the drunk parent, and perhaps needing to leave the house to pick up the drunk parent from bars or playing referee by not letting you see your other parent drunk. Your sober parent will probably be your most supportive one, while your drunk parent might not say kind things to you, especially while they are drunk. When your overdrinking parent is sober, they too can be a supportive parent in that moment, but when they start drinking, the switch could suddenly flip, which will just leave you feeling confused and frustrated.

Figure 8.1 *Being a teenager is hard enough these days. Having an overdrinking parent can complicate the stress and pressures you are already feeling especially when you can't find a quiet place in your own home that doesn't have shouting involved so you can just think or do your homework.* (Illustration by Kate Haberer).

Skeeter's Story

My mother was sick; she was also protecting me from my father when he would come home drunk. For whatever reason, my father thought it was a great idea to try and have a conversation with me late at night when he came home drunk after the bar closed. I would wake up often hearing my mom trying to stop my dad from walking down the hall to my room. You could smell the booze from my dad's clothes and his breath, and my mom was just trying to protect me from seeing him in that state. My mom was little, and my dad is a big guy, so he would always outmuscle her and I would get woken up. When they would wake me up, I would get so stressed out because I didn't want my parents fighting. I would get really tense and my heart would start to race. I would always have trouble going back to sleep. To this day, I struggle with sleeping, and I feel really uncomfortable when people are yelling near me.

My mother was always a kind, gentle, and supportive parent. I don't ever remember her losing patience with me or getting mad at me. My father, on the other hand, was a great dad when he was sober, but when he was drunk, he often made me cry. He broke my heart more times than I could count. When I would try to share my feelings the next day when he was sober, he would flat out deny what he did or said. He would tell me, "I didn't make you feel that way" or "I never said that" and would gaslight me. I always felt like I was walking on eggshells, and I became afraid of him. I never wanted to turn to him for advice because I was always afraid of if I'd end up talking to drunk dad instead of sober dad as I called it. Sober dad was a great dad who loved and supported me—drunk dad diminished my self-esteem during my whole childhood, never once apologized for drinking so much, never acknowledged or validated my feelings, never took responsibility for his actions, and would gaslight me and deny he said half the terrible things he said or half the terrible things he did. He's made me cry more than anyone ever in my life and he's my father.[1]

Ava's Story

The first memory that usually comes to mind is from when I was about eleven or twelve and she [my mom] had a job as a bartender at a little country, middle of nowhere, hole in the wall bar. She usually worked well past midnight and would come home during the early morning hours. On these nights, my stepdad was home with me and my siblings, but most of the time we were sleeping when she came home. One night, I just happened to wake up when she came home probably due to her loudness, but what I remember is poking my head out my bedroom and her sitting on the couch screaming about "spirits chasing" her and my stepdad yelling back at her that she was crazy and there were no spirits. He told her other things along the lines of "you had too much to drink" and "you must have had more than just alcohol, what drugs did you take?" He also questioned her about how late she had come home, so I guess it was later than she was supposed to be. Her excuse to being so late also pertained to "spirits chasing" her. I think she ended up passing out and my stepdad realized I had seen/heard their dispute and apologized to me for having to witness that and that my mom was so "crazy." My stepdad was mostly sober throughout my childhood, but only addressed my mom's problem every so often, and never took it far enough to get her actual help. They did fight a lot even when they both were sober, but either one of them drinking, especially my mom drinking or using drugs, always intensified their fights.[2]

Dilek's Story

My mother was sober, and she has never even tasted alcohol in her life. She hated alcohol because her four brothers and her dad never drank and to this day have never drunk alcohol, so my father's situation was a shock for my mother. She did not know what to do and how to handle the situation. They fought a lot for this reason. My mother was very passive when she was younger. She is far stronger, more outspoken and more confident right now but in the past, she was very passive and actually afraid of my father.[3]

Sarah's Story

My father was a very nice person. Too nice, in fact. He couldn't stand to leave my mom even though her drinking was severely affecting all of our lives. He worried that if he left her, she would kill herself, wouldn't survive, etc. He truly loved her unconditionally but couldn't find it in himself between working seven-day-a-week shifts to muster up the courage to do something about this. He was completely overwhelmed and ended up dying from a heart attack when I was seventeen. The stress got to him. Nonetheless, my dad was one of my very best friends in life and I miss him incredibly. I always feel guilty that when he died, I would tell my mother I wished it was her instead.[4]

I hope that you at least have a sober parent if you're dealing with an overdrinking parent. But if your sober parent is overwhelmed by your overdrinking parent's behavior then they might not be able to support you in the way that you need. Please reach out to another family member, a friend, your coach, your teacher—someone who is a positive supportive person in your life that can fully be there for you. You're going to need all of the support that you can get. It would be great if your overdrinking parent could just stop overdrinking so you could have a healthier childhood experience, but unless the overdrinking parent admits they have a problem and gets themselves some help, that could unfortunately be a long shot.

Megan's Story

My father used to describe Sober Mom and Drunk Mom to be as different as Dr. Jekyll and Mr. Hyde. When she drank, my sweet and kind mother transformed into an unrecognizable monster full of anger. If you met my mother, you wouldn't be able to imagine such a nice lady becoming so mean, but that is the power of alcohol and addiction. It makes good people act like terrible people. When drunk, my mother became loud and mad. She screamed and yelled at us over things that we had nothing to do with or had no control over. Most often, she

Figure 8.2 *Living with an overdrinking parent can be a confusing roller-coaster ride. One minute, your parent is caring, loving, and supportive, and the next minute they seem to care more about the bottle than they do your emotions and needs.* (Illustration by Kate Haberer).

appeared to have nothing real to be mad about so she simply mumbled nonsensical stuff.

She hurled insults to my father, sister and me—things she would have never said when sober that dug in and left scars on my soul. Even though I knew she was drunk when she said those things, it's not easy to forget such painful words. She was sometimes violent. One night, she threw a glass lamp across the room. She was most often violent toward my father—punching and shoving him. He was never violent in return; he tried to escape her as fast as possible. He put a lock on the basement door and stayed down there as his retreat.[5]

Veronica's Story

My sober parent, my mother, often fought with my father over his alcoholism and what it was doing to our family, amongst other things. Yes, my mother would tell my father that he had a problem, but it never reached him and even if it did, he was in denial.[6]

PART II

COPING WITH LIVING WITH AN OVERDRINKING PARENT

COPING WITH A PARENT WHO OVERDRINKS IS A PROCESS. IF your parent just stopped drinking tomorrow, life would be so much easier for everyone. But the reality is, the only person who can make your parent stop overdrinking is them. You have zero control of how much they do or don't drink. It is a choice they have to make within themselves to determine if they want to get help for their overdrinking or not. It's a process. They have to first admit they have a problem to themselves. Next, they will have to seek out help or counseling through rehabilitation. It's doable, but no one can make your overdrinking parent stop. So, you can daydream all you want that one day they will magically just stop drinking and life will get easier for you, but the reality is your overdrinking parent is most likely going to continue overdrinking. With that being said, having healthy ways for you to cope while living with your overdrinking parent is a must. In order for you to have a better future than you have been living in your current reality, learning to cope in healthy ways is essential. Coping in negative ways can absolutely destroy your future if you are not careful of the decisions you make today.

CHAPTER 9

Coping Methods

COPING WITH A PARENT WHO OVERDRINKS IS NOT GOING TO be an easy situation to deal with on a daily basis. Each young adult's situation is going to be different from another's, and each situation may have extenuating circumstances. You will have days when you are coping well with your parent's overdrinking and days when it will be a struggle. That's why you need to create a go-to playbook of positive coping strategies for yourself. In other words, have a list of activities you can do in case living with your overdrinking parent seems unbearable or beyond stressful. And you want to make sure that your coping methods are positive ones. The more positive ones you have, the more backups you can choose from if one activity isn't available. By having positive coping methods readily available for you, you are creating a positive outlet on hard days that will most likely arise from trying to deal with situations with your overdrinking parent.

REACH OUT
You might not have any other friends who also have an overdrinking parent like you do. And if you're coping with your overdrinking parent silently, either because you don't want other friends to know you have one, or because your family wants to keep your overdrinking parent situation private, reach out to those

who can offer you positive support. You can reach out to positive peers in your life and maybe take a break from your overdrinking parent and leave the house to go see a movie with your positive peer or go hang out at the mall together. Or you can reach out to a relative who is aware of the overdrinking parent who can give you a safe space to open up and talk about your feelings. You might have a sober parent you can talk to as well. Reaching out can give you a positive outlet so you can cope, vent, take a break, or de-stress in a healthy way, which is important for your mental health and overall well-being.

SEEK COUNSELING AND SUPPORT GROUPS
Counseling can be beneficial to coping with an overdrinking parent. Guidance on how to navigate this trying situation from someone supportive on the outside can really help you, especially on those really complicated days. You can seek counseling through your school, your job, or through your health insurance. Check out the resources section in the back of this book. Al-Anon and Alateen are fantastic go-to support groups.

Georgianne's Story
I did attend a few Al-Anon meetings, but it wasn't for me at the time; however, I have had a lot of counseling over the years.[1]

Sarah's Story
I have attended therapy and read many self-help books. Seeing a licensed counselor was the best decision I could have made.[2]

PLAY SPORTS
Playing sports is a really healthy and great way to de-stress and let out some of that frustration that might build up when you're trying to deal with an overdrinking parent at home. Your home is supposed to provide safety and comfort, but an overdrinking parent can cause you stress when you are there. Getting out of the

house—even if it's just to your backyard to shoot hoops or play catch, or taking a jog around the neighborhood—has a highly beneficial reward for you.

Skeeter's Story

I was on the basketball team during middle school and high school. I also played softball and ran track and played volleyball on the school teams. You could find me either riding my bike or I was usually at the park everyday with my friends playing some sort of sports. Some people like to sit on the couch and watch sports—I was the one who was always playing them. I always thought I was just a jock and that's why, but looking back I think I was playing sports as a method of positive coping for my overdrinking parent. Sports kept me busy, and it kept me out of the house. Exercise is great against stress and so I used it as a healthy and positive coping method.[3]

READ A BOOK

Reading can take you far away from the life you are forced to live. You can get lost in far-off castles, or suddenly be on a beach in Hawaii, or meet some new characters. There are also books that deal with what you're struggling with in real life. Whether fiction or nonfiction, books can be an escape if you need one, and can be used as a positive coping mechanism to try and navigate the situation involving your overdrinking parent. Bibliotherapy is how we can use books as a way to cope with a stressful occurrence in our life. Relating to fictional characters who are navigating a situation like yours can help you feel less alone, and you can gain some ideas or perspective on how to navigate your nonfiction situation.

VOLUNTEER

Sometimes serving others before serving ourselves can be very therapeutic and healing. Sometimes we get stuck in our worries and stresses and we tend to forget there are people out in the world who have more problems than we do. By helping others who are struggling, you can take the focus off of what you are dealing with and also genuinely put other people before yourself. Check out your local church, your school, community center, or local nonprofit organizations to seek out volunteer opportunities.

Whichever positive coping method you choose, make sure it is the one that is best for *you*. You are the best person to know what it is that *you* truly need.

WRITE OUT YOUR FEELINGS

Writing can be very therapeutic when dealing with a parent who overdrinks. You can write a letter to your overdrinking parent about all the things you would like to say to them (up to you if you hand them the letter or not). You can write a fictional story that has characters based on what you are dealing with. You can write a poem about your feelings. You can write to God, your aunt, your friend, whomever. Writing has no limits. Ava said she writes about her childhood often and considers it therapeutic and healing. She even wrote a short story titled "Mama Had a Bad Day" to help her cope. Here is an excerpt from that story:

Mama didn't come home again tonight. Granny told me Mama is having a bad day and Pawpaw said it's okay because he and Granny love me and are going to take care of me. I took a bath and Granny brushed my hair.

I asked her where mama was and she said, "I really don't know darling, but she will be here in the morning, okay?"

"Okay," but I knew even if she was home in the morning, she would stay asleep and not want to see me.

Granny tucked me in, and I looked around at my walls trying not to cry. I have to be a big girl. I stared out the window until I fell asleep hoping I would see mama's car pull into the driveway.

***

Just as I expected, Mama didn't want to wake up to tell me bye before school. Granny fixed me breakfast and helped me get dressed, but Mama just stayed in bed. I wondered if my classmates' grandmas would help them get ready for school. Probably not because I bet their mamas get up with them in the morning.

I watched TV with Pawpaw until the school bus came and hoped Mama would wake up before I had to go, but she never did.

When I got home, Mama was gone again. Granny helped me with my homework, and I did all my chores so I could play for a while. We ate dinner and Granny read me a book. I learned to tell time so I would know when Mama might be home from work. The big hand was on the six and the little hand was on the seven so she should be home any minute now.

I heard the back door open, and I jumped up and yelled, "MAMA!"

She gave me a big hug and said, "Hey baby, let's go in the living room. We have to tell you and Granny and Pawpaw some news."[4]

NEGATIVE COPING METHODS

Sometimes when you're going through a stressful situation such as trying to cope with an overdrinking parent, the stress can build up and overcloud your judgment. It can steer you into making decisions that aren't healthy and that you normally wouldn't make. Sometimes making unhealthy choices feels easier during a stressful time, like an easy way to cope with something. But before you make the easy choice, know that nothing worth doing is easy. Think before you act. Think about the aftermath and the consequences before you make decisions, for some decisions you make on impulse can have negative life-changing effects.

Underage Drinking

The worst thing you can do is drink to try and deal with your overdrinking parent's drinking. If you are underage, that can also cause a lot of harm for your future. You can get arrested and charged, you can lose college scholarships, you can get a DUI (driving under the influence), you can hurt yourself or hurt others—the list goes on and on as to why drinking is a bad idea. If you are over twenty-one, remember to identify your addiction genetic components to be careful going down a drinking path. Know the law and what a healthy serving size for a drink is. Never drink and drive.

Drugs and Other Substances
Trying to cope with your overdrinking parent's behavior by using drugs and other substances is going to just harm you even more. Remember, if overdrinking is in your DNA and you have a family history of this, that means there is a higher chance you can get addicted if you try something. So please remember that the first drug you attempt could be your last drug—if you get what I mean. It is not worth throwing your life away over. Especially nowadays, unless you get a prescription from a legal pharmacy, how do you even know what you are really taking?

Risky Sexual Behavior
Having multiple partners or "sleeping around" to try and cope with stress from your everyday life can also create more difficulties in your life. This is not the answer either. Having sex is a serious and important decision. Make sure you are making decisions with a level head and not trying to just escape your reality. Your decision today can give you a new reality tomorrow.

Self-Harm and Suicide
If you cannot handle what is going on at home with your parent's overdrinking behavior, please reach out to a trusted adult who can give you a safe space immediately. Don't wait any longer for things to get worse. Reach out to your sober parent, a sober family member, a teacher, a coach, your pastor, or a national hotline number—so you can get the immediate help you need, especially

if you have been self-harming or having suicidal thoughts. There are tons of resources out there and people who care about you. Please reach out instead of trying to hold everything in. Look at the back of this book for important contact numbers. Help is available.

Ava's Story

When I was in middle and high school, I unfortunately did turn to some negative coping mechanisms. I self-harmed from thirteen to sixteen and struggled with prescription medication and suicidal thoughts all the way up until eighteen. At eighteen, I hit rock bottom and ended up with a seventy-two-hour hold in a psych ward, which sent me to my knees and giving it all back to God. I fully credit my relationship with Christ for how healed I am today. It took realizing that I can't get through this life on my own and now I walk with Him. I do have positive coping mechanisms which mostly consist of prayer and reading my Bible as well as journaling time to time and even crying once in a while. Having strong and trusting relationships with other people that also trust in God also helps tremendously. I often confide in my now fiancé as well as my grandmother. I have several trusted individuals through my church and a couple of best friends and family members that have great listening ears on my bad days. I definitely still get sad and even frustrated sometimes when I think about my mom, but I understand how much of it is out of my control and that those negative feelings won't bring her back into my life or make her a better person.[5]

Remember that dealing with your overdrinking parent is just a temporary situation. If you're dealing with an overdrinking parent and you're about to graduate from high school and move away to college, your living situation is about to change. You won't have to deal with your overdrinking parent twenty-four/seven anymore because you won't be living at home—you'll be living on campus somewhere else. If you come back and visit during the holidays or during the summertime, you might be exposing yourself to your overdrinking parent for a short time, but soon your living situation might get less stressful for you. And when you visit, you don't have to move back in, or even stay in the same house for that matter, with your overdrinking parent and relive everything all over again. You can live or stay with other relatives or friends instead or rent an apartment or a house to distance yourself. It's tricky when you're under eighteen because you can't move out on your own just yet and you might have limited alternatives. If your situation is beyond unbearable, and you can't move in with other friends or family members, you do have a legal option of emancipation. Emancipation is when you're under eighteen but you want to legally separate yourself from your parents. You can present your case to the judge in a local court that you no longer want your parents to have custody over you and that you want to have your own custody. In many ways that can free you from your overdrinking parent if the situation is beyond unbearable.

Don't cope in a negative way. Don't give in to peer pressure from your friends to drink underage, or excessively if you are older, just as a way to cope with your parent's overdrinking. You of all people know firsthand that is not a good decision to make. Don't go down the same path that you are frustrated with your overdrinking parent for going down. Recognize that your parent has a problem, a problem that you cannot solve for them, and learn from their behavior and their mistakes. Stay away from peers who try and steer you down a path like this. Stay away from drugs. Don't cope negatively because your life can take a turn for the worse. Don't let your parent's mistakes and negative life choices cloud your judgment. You know deep down that they are not living in a healthy way and not making healthy decisions. Following in their footsteps and doing the exact same thing they are will only lead you to become exactly like them—overdrinking and all. You *do* have a choice. Make the right one. When you come to that proverbial fork in the road, choose the good path, the non-overdrinking path—not the bad overdrinking path. I promise you will thank yourself later.

The Importance of Support

IN DIFFICULT TIMES, IN PARENTAL OVERDRINKING TIMES, FINDING support is key to getting through a challenging situation. Support can look like many different things: a friend who lets you vent about your overdrinking parent; an Al-Anon or Alateen support group that can give you that safe space to realize you are not dealing with this alone; a helpful book or movie that features an overdrinking parent; a sober parent to talk to. And so much more. Support comes in many different forms, and the beauty is you get to seek out support that works best for you.

SUPPORT GROUPS

Support groups are beneficial because the people who attend are there for reasons similar to yours. It helps you see real people and hear real stories of what they are going through in their lives. Some of their circumstances might be different than yours, but hearing others share their stories can give you a different perspective on your own story. There are some support groups that are specifically for you, the nondrinker, to learn how to cope with an overdrinking parent. Al-Anon and Alateen are two wonderfully supportive groups to check out (see the resources in the back of this book for further information). Other support groups can come from nonprofit organizations, resources from your counselor, through the local hospital, or even through your church or community center.

Megan's Story

When I was twenty-six years old, I felt hopeless and dreaded every day. I knew I couldn't go on for the rest of my life feeling like that, but I felt I had no way out. I felt that I had been handed a life sentence of being completely wrapped up in the chaos that surrounded my mother's substance use disorder. I felt wholly responsible for the well-being of my younger sister and cleaning up the messes for our father and mother that resulted from the drinking. At that point, I did the bravest thing that I've ever done in my life which was to attend my first Al-Anon meeting. I arrived at the meeting believing I was there still seeking a solution to my mother's problem.

But as each attendee shared their story, I recognized my own story. I thought, that's how I feel! I realized that I wasn't there for my mother. I was there for me. My whole life, I had been focused on solving a problem that wasn't mine and through that process, I had become ill myself and I was no longer living. I cleared my throat, sat up tall, and shared my story with the room full of strangers. It was the start of my life-changing healing journey.

For several years, I regularly attended Al-Anon meetings. I read every book that I could find about addiction and its effects on families. I searched online for blogs or content from fellow adult children of alcoholics. I could find very few, so I started writing about it myself. Sharing my story of healing and connecting with others who have experienced similar life stories has been extremely cathartic for me. I also began seeing a therapist. Through this focus on education and healing, I finally had enough clarity to learn what self-care truly is. I started living a life how I want to live life. That was fifteen years ago. Today, I love my life. I am living proof that it is possible to create a future life that you can't even imagine today if you are living with an overdrinker. I'm so grateful for all the resources and the people who shared their stories with me.[1]

Veronica's Story

I regret not contacting Alateen when I was a teenager as I was not aware of this extended service for teens. The behavior and anything that can consist of, was so normalized in my home I did not conceive of reaching out for help nor did I have that great of a support network. I started to attend therapy in my mid-late teens where I started to exhibit emotional and mental health difficulties, and I still am in therapy.[2]

FAMILY SUPPORT

If you have a sober parent, they might be a good form of support to open up and share your feelings about your overdrinking parent to. However, in some cases, your sober parent might be overwhelmed by your overdrinking parent, so that might not be the best option. Your siblings, especially older ones, can be a great form of support for you to vent and open up to, because they are most likely living in the same house and are experiencing difficulties with your overdrinking parent as well. Reaching out to family members that can give you a safe space to get out of the home you share with your overdrinking parent and to vent about the situation is another helpful idea for seeking support. Sometimes if you are dealing with an overdrinking parent, family members know, but friends and neighbors might not. Family can be very helpful, and they know the overdrinker on a more personal level—that is, the overdrinker could be your aunt's brother or sister, for example.

Megan's Story

My mother isolated us from her family and my father's family. Fortunately, I grew very close with my grandmother on my father's side who turned into quite a supporter for me. Around twelve years old, I made the effort to build those relationships. I feel grateful for my grandmother and others in my family who recognized what was going on and really became people I could rely on. But that didn't happen until I was old enough to kind of build those relationships myself.[3]

School Support

Finding support at your school, whether it be your high school or college, can be highly beneficial as well. Reach out to your school counselor, your teacher, or your coach to whom you can likely vent to about what you are dealing with at home. They can also probably provide you with resources to help you through this. An idea is maybe your counselor can put a mini peer support group together that can remain private for you and some of your other peers who might all be experiencing an overdrinking parent at home, so you all don't feel like you are dealing with the situation alone.

Employee Assistance Program at Your Job

For those of you who are working, check out your health plan to see what counseling services might be offered through your insurance. If you are still living at home, then your sober parent can check your health insurance benefits. But also check out your job's Employee Assistance Program, or EAP for short. Some employers offer a couple of free counseling sessions that can help get you started or even save you some money on those first couple of sessions.

As you can see, you have many different options about seeking out helpful support. Just remember to choose the right method of support that works for *you*. You might just want to vent alone in your room by writing in a diary, or drawing or painting, or by listening to music or creating your own lyrics. You know yourself and the activities you like. If others aren't around to offer support at the exact moment you are looking for some, look within to be there for yourself by engaging in positive, constructive activities you enjoy. This will help you cope with your overdrinking parent's often challenging behavior.

Finding Support for Your Overdrinking Parent

You love your parent despite their overdrinking. But remember you cannot force them to get help. They have to make that decision for themselves. Nevertheless, families will still try to encourage the overdrinker to get help by way of such things as planning an intervention, calling a doctor or rehab center, or encouraging them to go to AA (Alcoholics Anonymous) meetings. A lot of times these attempts are unsuccessful, but sometimes they plant seeds that give lifelines later on to help the overdrinking parent. Each family is different and has different circumstances.

Veronica's Story

My mom, brother, and I would try to get him to attend AA, but it is not something that can be forced. My father was often in denial when the worst was happening, but now, he can admit it.[4]

CHAPTER 11

Ongoing Psychological Effects

IF YOU ARE IN A SITUATION WHERE YOU CANNOT LIVE WITH another relative, move out, or separate your living situation from that of your overdrinking parent, hopefully you are finding healthy outlets to help you cope for the time being. The situation is not ideal, but I hope you are finding support and keeping yourself around caring people while you are trying to navigate all of this. If your overdrinking parent drinks a lot in the late afternoon or early evening, I hope you are able to somehow distance yourself from their negative behavior. If you are not able to distance yourself from their bad behavior, then its effects might start to stress your out even more. Depending on whether they are saying hurtful words to you, getting physical, or being more neglectful—these effects can take a toll on your mental and psychological health. Again, please try to find as much support as you can during this, so you are not dealing with it alone. You are still very young and have a lot on your plate already; dealing with an overdrinking parent is just going to add unneeded stress in your life. Get into school counseling sessions or employer-offered counseling sessions, talk to your sober parent or kind and patient relative, or join an Al-Anon or Alateen support group to help you with this. The more you are exposed to the overdrinking parent, the more the psychological effects can hinder your overall well-being and mental health.

CODEPENDENCY

According to Merriam-Webster, the definition of codependency is a psychological condition or a relationship in which a person manifesting low self-esteem and a strong desire for approval has an unhealthy attachment to another often controlling or manipulative person (such as a person with an addiction to alcohol or drugs). Codependency tendencies and an overdrinking parent often can come hand in hand. The overdrinking parent can often be controlling or manipulative, especially in their drunken state. As children, teenagers, and even young adults, there is a natural longing and desire to want to bond with your parent. So, children often look to their parents for approval. In this situation, you are trying to get approval from an overdrinking parent who is not making parenting their first and foremost priority—which they should be. Therefore, your self-esteem can be played with, especially when your overdrinking parent is in their drunken state. When they are sober, they can be the best, most supportive parent in the world. But when they are drunk, they can turn into a hurtful and manipulative parent, all while tugging at your heartstrings. If they were anyone else but your parent, you might recognize that this is toxic behavior, and so you would know to distance yourself from that person. Yet, how does that work when the toxic person you are trying to distance yourself from is your parent who you will always naturally want to bond with and seek approval from? It is not that simple. This is where codependency comes in. You have a parent–child relationship with your overdrinking parent. When they mistreat you, you might struggle with distancing yourself from them and their bad behavior because, underneath the toxicity, they are still your parent. It rocks the very foundation of your relationship as parent and child with your overdrinking parent and it's like a game of tug and war.

Skeeter's Story

I struggle with my relationship with my overdrinking father. I can't tell you how many times someone has dropped the accusatory phrase of "you are a codependent" in my lap over the years. It frustrates me because I try not to do it, but in my case, my father is my only living parent—which makes this task of distancing myself from him so much harder. I lost my mother when I was a little girl, so of course, naturally, I was going to become really attached to my still living father. The fact that he has been an overdrinker since before my mother died makes me feel like I am a codependent in the deepest way—something I struggle to break free from. How do you distance yourself from your sometimes toxic overdrinking father when he is the only parent you have left? Welcome to my life. If you have the answer to this, please share it with me.[1]

Megan's Story
My father did not have a substance use disorder. However, he was deeply codependent and did not have proper education about how to handle my mother's disorder and the effects of it on our family. He passed away ten years ago, just as I was beginning to help educate him as I made my way on my healing journey. I wish he could have become more educated earlier in life so that our family would not have suffered from the effects of my mother's substance use disorder so much.

My father was a classic codependent and wrapped up in the chaos of my mother's addiction. He loved my mother, my sister and me very deeply. He was an optimistic person by nature and lacked any education about how to handle addiction in the family. He always seemed to believe that things would have a way of working out. He held on to hope that one day my mother would just miraculously stop drinking.

He tried to stop her from having the ability to buy alcohol, from taking away all her money to even disabling her vehicle. He didn't believe that she could stop drinking without help but he didn't believe that any intervention or efforts to get her to go to a rehabilitation program would be successful. My father knew my mother's post-traumatic stress disorder and deep childhood wounds would require intensive therapy for healing. Since my mother was not willing to go through

Figure 11.1 *You depend on your parents to provide you food, clothing, a roof over your head, education, health care, nurturing, and safety. It is not fair or morally right to you that they are sitting there buying beer and being unavailable to you while your basic needs such as having enough food in the house are not being met because of their drunkenness.* (Illustration by Kate Haberer).

that process despite his urging, he did not believe that she would ever achieve recovery from her substance use disorder.[2]

Jody Lamb's Expert Insight on Codependency

Jody Lamb, author, speaker, and advocate, shares her expert insight when it comes to teenagers becoming codependents.

The role switcheroo with a parent who overdrinks goes hand in hand with what the experts call "codependency." When you become codependent, you become completely absorbed with someone else's problems and you do lots of things to try to solve those problems, even though they are not yours to solve. Though you may realize you cannot control another parent's overdrinking, you may spend a lot of time thinking or worrying about their drinking and strategizing ways to make them drink less often. In a household where a parent is overdrinking, codependency actions could show up as dumping out alcohol bottles to prevent the parent from drinking, being quiet and "walking on eggshells" when the parent is around, trying to avoid situations that could upset your parent or cause them to drink more, being as "perfect" as you can at school or sports to please your parent or breaking up arguments between your siblings to prevent your parent having to deal with it. It can also show up as making excuses for the parent who overdrinks and hiding things they do or do not do from other people.

Codependency is a normal reaction to what you've experienced. Taking care of your parent's responsibilities and related behavior becomes second nature because it may be the only way of life you've ever known if your parent has been overdrinking since you were a little kid. Over time, as you take on more responsibilities for your parent who overdrinks, you may even begin to enjoy the sense of being so needed. It may give you a sense of control—something you may have longed for your whole life.

If you're wrapped up in codependency, the first step to freeing yourself is to recognize that your only job in life is to take good care of you. You cannot control someone else's drinking, you cannot cure them of their dependence on alcohol, and you don't have any ability to cause it or minimize it. You are a separate person who can only control you. Your parent's overdrinking is part of their personal journey. It is up to them to get help and take care of themselves. Healing from codependency may mean you have to stop taking care of your parent's responsibilities or covering up for their mistakes that result from their drinking. This may feel wrong at first, but looking back, it may have been life changing.[3]

GUILT

Guilt is what teenagers and young adults of overdrinkers can feel on a regular basis. Guilt from feeling embarrassed and ashamed of your overdrinking parent. Guilt from hiding that you have an overdrinking parent or maybe even telling white lies to your friends to cover your overdrinking parent's behavior. Guilt from trying to love your overdrinking parent just like other teens do with their "normal" non-overdrinking parents, but sometimes resenting them for the daily roller-coaster ride of emotions they have put you through for months and perhaps even years. Guilt from the scene your overdrinking parent caused at the movie theater, restaurant, or your school.

Guilt is very present in households with an overdrinking parent. Most overdrinking parent households are considered chaotic and dysfunctional. And let's not forget the guilt when your overdrinking parent lashes out at you—then the next day when they are sober, denies that their outburst ever happened—to where now you have entered a potential gaslighting stage with your overdrinking parent. Gaslighting, according to Merriam-Webster, is to psychologically manipulate (a person) usually over an extended period of time so that the victim questions the validity of their own thoughts, perception of reality, or memories and experiences confusion, loss of confidence and self-esteem, and doubts concerning their own emotional or mental stability. For example, one night your overdrinking parent can cause a huge scene at the grocery store and get kicked out and, the next day, deny any of it happened and accuse you of remembering the situation incorrectly. This messes with your own personal thoughts and reality, and you start to question if you really did remember the situation correctly—is your overdrinking parent right and you forgot what really happened?

Skeeter's Story

One night, I picked my father up after he had been drinking, and he left his car at the bar until the next day. I had to work early in the morning, and he had me pick him up really late. I was exhausted when I woke up and had to head into work. On my way out the door, he stopped me and said that he wanted to take my car since his was still at the bar and that he would drop me off at work. Sick and tired of the exhausting routine, I put my foot down and told him no. I felt like he was treating me like a child when I had been parenting him more than he had been parenting me! He is not used to anyone on the planet ever telling him the word "no." I told him that he decided to drink, which was his choice, and that he could call a taxi to go pick up his car at the bar himself. I needed my car to go to work—I was an adult at that point, and I was being responsible by going to my job. It wasn't my fault that he decided to drink too much at the bar, which resulted in him leaving his car and not having access to transportation.

I had never stood up to my father in my whole entire life. I felt so empowered and confident in my decision. I was proud of myself. And then that lasted for fifteen seconds. Because no one ever tells my father no, that word triggered a side of my father I had never seen in my life. He quickly became enraged with me. He got very close to my face and started screaming and yelling at me to where spit and saliva started spraying out of his mouth. He started going off on me that I was selfish and on my high horse and he was my father, and I shouldn't treat him this way. That was the first and only time in my whole life I ever was worried my father was about to hit me. He didn't, but what he said next stung me for many years. He said I was a bitch and that I was nothing like my late mother. For if my late mother was still alive, she would have done what he asked, and driven him/let him take her car for the day. I, his daughter, on the other hand, stood up to him and told him "no," and that's why he said what he did.

That was the day I moved out of my father's house forever, and I stayed with another relative temporarily until I found my own place. Looking back, that was the best decision I could have made, and I have no regrets. That was the last day I ever lived and will ever live with my overdrinking father ever again.

Months later when my father was sober for a minute, I tried talking to him about that day and how what he said was extremely hurtful. He flat out denied that he would ever say anything hurtful like that to me in his life. So not only did he destroy my insides when he said those hurtful words about me and to me but denying them later felt like he invalidated my feelings, which was as bad or worse than calling me a bitch and saying that I was nothing like my beautiful late mother. My father has broken my heart more times than I can count, but that moment was the most hurtful one. That's when I discovered gaslighting, which led me to realize that he had been doing that to me for years.[4]

Ava's Story

My mom always said hurtful things to me, my stepdad, my grandparents, my siblings, my real dad, and so on whether she was sober or drunk. The insults were definitely harsher when she was under the influence. I did, however, witness her being physically abusive to my stepfather on more than one occasion. She also was very verbally and mentally (manipulative, liar, narcissistic, selfish, insulting) abusive all of the time to all of us.[5]

Codependency. Guilt. Gaslighting. These are what we consider negative words that represent negative situations. They can all be present for young adults—in this case, you, the reader—when you live with an overdrinking parent. Please always remember that your overdrinking parent's overdrinking problems are not your fault. You neither cause them nor fuel them. You are not alone in this. Through support, time, and healing, you can get through this. Living at home with your overdrinking parent is temporary. This will not last forever and you will get a shot at living a better life. Look forward to the future.

MOVIE BREAK: *RENFIELD*

In the movie *Renfield* starring Nicolas Cage and Nicholas Hoult, Dracula (played by Nicolas Cage) is sucking the life out of his "companion," Renfield (played by Nicholas Hoult). It takes time for Renfield to learn this, but he eventually realizes that Dracula treats him terribly and their relationship is toxic. So Renfield seeks out a support group. The support group empowers Renfield so he can turn his life around, he can heal from the mistreatment by Dracula over the years—the gaslighting, the shaming, the guilt, and the codependent negative relationship they have. Renfield gains courage and breaks away from Dracula. Then Dracula finds out that Renfield started a new life without him. Dracula finds his new place and basically sucks Renfield back into his world again, and the new life that Renfield created away from Dracula is destroyed by Dracula all over again.[6]

The story of Renfield is how you might feel with your overdrinking parent. Each time you get the courage to distance yourself from them, or set healthy boundaries, or really make progress with healing, they suck you back in again. As frustrating as that is, don't stop trying. This is when you can also pull out your positive coping methods playbook and talk to a caring person, attend a support group meeting, or even volunteer to try and fight back in a positive way during this incredibly frustrating time.

Skeeter shares her frustrations with her overdrinking father,

If I ask him for space, he will tell me how to feel and say, "You don't need space from me. I am your father." If I stop answering his calls or texts, he sends the police to my house to do a welfare check on me. When I talk to family and friends to see if anyone else can have a talk with my overdrinking father to back off, he manipulates what I tell everyone else and turns them against me—like says that I am going through something. If I ignore his calls, he calls nonstop through the night. If I don't answer my front door, he stops by unannounced and rings it [the doorbell] incessantly until I answer it. Then days later acts like everything is okey dokey.

I feel like I am sentenced to life in prison and the warden is my overdrinking father. I have tried to have heart-to-heart talks over the years about his behavior, but he just denies he says or does things or has a drinking problem. I feel like the only way I can break free from him is after he dies one day. I know the way that sounds, but our relationship is toxic. I love him unconditionally, but he refuses to let me heal and move forward with my life. I already lost my mother when I was young, but I have been dealing with my overdrinking father for longer than that. Will I ever get to live my life and actually try to enjoy it, free from all of this?

NEGLECT

Sadly, this one might hit a lot more of you. Neglect in a house with an overdrinking parent is more common than not. After all, the overdrinking parent might also be the one in charge of going grocery shopping or paying the bills. If you have two overdrinking parents at home, this might be a little worse for you. Sometimes the overdrinking parent puts their overdrinking "want" over what their family's true "needs" are. They are just concentrating on overdrinking and are not noticing that their teenagers need food, or they might skip out on paying a bill and incur late fees—but they have plenty to buy everyone a round at the bar that week. It is irresponsible and should not be happening, but for some of you, it happens anyway. Neglect is when your overdrinking parent is not taking care of you, their child, as they responsibly should be.

Skeeter's Story

An awful, toxic idea, but my father thought it would be a great idea to buy a bar on the other side of town shortly after he moved us away from the home we shared with our late mother in another state. Not surprisingly, it just added more complications to his preexisting overdrinking problems.

The bar was located, in my opinion, in a ghetto part of town. Keep in mind I was twelve at the time. My father would be gone at the bar working all week long. He was able to obtain a discount at a nearby hotel close to the bar that he would just stay at instead of coming home to help save him time and gas money. My brother started working at the bar as well, another huge mistake as he was just fifteen years old.

My dad would come home Sundays after work, reload his clothes, leave me some money to get groceries (sometimes), and take off again. There was no one there to make me dinner. There was no one there to drive me to school. There was no one there to help me with my homework. There was no one there to talk to. There was no one there for anything. It was like I lived alone at twelve years old.

Sometimes my dad would forget to leave me money and he would forget to go grocery shopping. When I would call him out on it, he would tell me I was overreacting. He would then open the pantry and try to prove to me there was plenty of food. Feeling defeated, he would walk away, and I would just stare at the pantry, as the "plenty of food" was lots of containers filled with baking soda or cornstarch or sugar. It wasn't food for a teenager but just baking supplies.

When I was getting tired of the situation and after many nights of tears, I tried to get brave one day. I was writing a letter during the summer that I was going to mail to my friend. I was brave enough to tell her about my situation at home with my dad and I told her how sometimes he didn't leave me any food. But my letter got intercepted on the family computer and I got in so much trouble to where my dad gaslighted me and said what I wrote wasn't true. He deleted my letter. That letter was my cry for help to try and tell someone what was really going on. I got in so much trouble for "lying" that I was too scared to try and reach out to someone else ever again. That day I accepted that things weren't going to get better and that I just had to accept that I was going to continue being treated that way.

Looking back, I wish I knew about emancipation. I felt like my father didn't care or love me. That he was so selfish during my childhood because he was just thinking about himself. He made sure all his time was spent at the bar, that money was going to have the "lifestyle" he wanted; going to fancy restaurants, etcetera . . . but he couldn't spend more time trying to take care of me. I felt so alone and so unloved while I was still grieving the death of my mother.[7]

Emancipation is when you are legally released from your parents' care. This means that if you are in an awful situation with your overdrinking parent or parents, and you don't have someone sober in the family who can take care of you instead, and things are just so unlivable and toxic that it's affecting your everyday life and needs, emancipation could be an option for you. You have to go through your local court system to file paperwork to legally and officially emancipate yourself. In other words, if your emancipation is granted, you are releasing your parent from being legally bound to take care of you prior to reaching eighteen years old. With this being said, don't take this decision lightly. You will have to have income to support yourself and a job and to supply yourself with a roof over your head or make sure you have arrangements made. Once your parent is legally released from being financially responsible for taking care of you, you have to take care of yourself. You can't expect your parent to pay for an apartment for you or even provide you food after you have been emancipated. It is not a situation to be taken lightly. You need to make sure that you have a financial plan for how to support yourself after the decision is legal and final.

Sarah's Story

My life was hell. My clothes always reeked of her cigarette smell. I had no food to eat, no one to help guide me after school. My mother would abandon me for days on end.[8]

MOVIE BREAK: *ANGELA'S ASHES*

In the 1999 movie *Angela's Ashes*, Frankie is a young boy who has an overdrinking, unemployed father. When the father does get money, he spends it on alcohol instead of taking care of his family. The family is already living in poverty, and they have already suffered a tragedy.[9]

TRUST ISSUES

Children trust their parents wholeheartedly to feed them, provide for them, meet their basic life needs, provide safety, maintain a stable home, and show them love. When there's an overdrinking parent or two involved in the household situation, trust can be broken, especially if a child's basic needs are not being met. Is the overdrinking parent helping their child with their homework or are they always drunk? Did the overdrinking parent spend all the grocery money on alcohol? Is the overdrinking parent passed out on the couch instead of attending the child's important game that night? All these little misses due to alcohol can really add up and can break the trust between a child and their parent. A bond between a child and a parent is a lifelong, important one, and shaking that bond due to the ups and downs of an overdrinking parent can cause the child to develop trust issues—not just with their parents but also with relationships and friendships—and to have difficulty bonding with people.

Skeeter's Story

I remember as a child how much I loved both of my parents. As I started getting older, I think I began to suddenly sense that my little childhood world was not as perfect as I thought it was. Of course I was naive, but around five years old, little did I know, my foundation that I felt safe in started to shake. Suddenly I was aware that my father was an overdrinker and that my mother was seriously ill. Suddenly my safety net started getting little holes in it. My mother got sicker, and my father continued to drink, so every day started being different than before. When I thought everything was settling down or getting back to normal, a curve ball would happen—my mother would wake us up at 2 a.m. to have to go pick up my father who was drunk from a bar. We were too young for her to leave us home alone in the middle of the night, so we'd have to get woken up and get in the car to go find my father (who would be often hiding in the bushes to get away from the police who would be looking for him). Or my mother had a seizure right in front of me and the ambulance had to be called one day. I saw them take her away from our home unconscious. I was a stressed-out kid living in a now dysfunctional environment. Years later and I struggle with trusting those closest to me. I guess you can say I'm still waiting every day for the other shoe to drop in my life. If anyone makes a tiny mistake, it makes me go into overdrive of not trusting people all over again. Since my mother died and my father chose the bottle over me a long time ago, I struggle with trusting that

I'm truly in real loving relationships and friendships now. I struggle with trusting people because in my childhood those who I should have been able to count on the most—trust—who were supposed to give me safety and love in many ways left me. I felt abandoned—really badly two times—once after my mother died, and the second when I realized I was never going to be more important than the bottle in my father's eyes.[10]

ANXIETY

Anxiety is common in dysfunctional overdrinking parent households. Knowing that the parent is on their way home coming back from a bar late at night is like a routine to prepare for. You know how your overdrinking parent is about to behave, so it's like you mentally prepare your body to be in fight-or-flight mode. You might try to avoid them and stay in your room because you know it will feel like a "walking on eggshells" environment. Or you start having a panic attack because each time your parent overdrinks, they come home and throw furniture around, break dishes in the kitchen, yell at you, or hit other family members. Anxiety is another psychological side effect of living with an overdrinking parent at home.

Veronica's Story

My parent's alcoholism affected my childhood in the sense that it contributed and exacerbated anxieties that I had and other emotional difficulties. The emotional and sporadic physical absence of my father deeply impacted me and my internal foundation of myself. I continue to learn and realize each day how my father's alcoholism has affected my family and I. There are still difficulties that I face, and it is not always easy to give myself the compassion that I needed when I was younger.[11]

DEPRESSION

Feeling depressed can really affect your day-to-day life and overall mental well-being. Knowing the situation you are in, whether you can tell someone, do anything about it or not, or feel like you are stuck in the situation until you can move out—those doom-like feelings can leave you feeling incredibly depressed. Even seeing a loving family walking around the mall together smiling and showing love to each other can trigger you to feel depressed because you start comparing your family to theirs and you can feel the difference. If you are having depressive thoughts and they are increasing, please talk to a trusted adult so you can gain access to a doctor or counselor who can help walk you through feeling depressed.

POST-TRAUMATIC STRESS DISORDER

Some situations might arise that will take you extra time to work through and recover from, even more than you are already dealing with of the simple fact you are being exposed to an overdrinking parent's negative behavior. Maybe one night, after your parent came home from a bar, things got really bad. Perhaps your overdrinking parent was physical with you to where it did severe damage to your overall health or well-being and now you are struggling with post-traumatic stress disorder (PTSD) from it. You will definitely need support in navigating this and processing what happened. Again, please reach out to a trusted adult who can help point you in the right direction to seek out a counselor or someone who is credentialed in the medical field to assist you.

STRESS

Stress is usually present for everyone involved in an overdrinking parental household. There's stress from anticipating the mood they are going to be in, from having to walk on eggshells, from worrying that neighbors will hear all the yelling, from expecting them to make yet another scene—the list is endless. Stress is not good for children, teenagers, or young adults—or even adults, for that matter. A little life stress is normal, and eustress (positive stress) can be motivational, but negative stress felt in an overbearing way in your childhood can lead to potential struggles in your adulthood if not worked on with a counselor. To be in a constant state of stress is not good for your mental or even physical health.

Megan's Story

My whole world crumbled whenever my mother was drunk. My stomach was the first to react with instant knots, followed by my entire body tightening up when I detected the familiar slur in her speech. I was often unable to sleep during the night because my mother would binge drink into the early morning hours. I feared that she would burn down the house while we were sleeping, so I wouldn't sleep. There was good reason to fear this, as multiple times she left food cooking on the stove, passed out, and the house smoke detectors went off.

I felt it was my responsibility to take care of everyone in the house yet was unable to control their safety. My mother became very angry and nonsensical. She would often mumble for hours to herself as if she were completely out of her mind. Then she'd wake up the next morning and a very happy upbeat and pleasant mood as if nothing had happened. This roller coaster of calm and turmoil became very draining for me over the years.

It was difficult to concentrate on my homework, especially when I got to the high school level. I always took care of my younger sister, making sure that she had enough to eat and that everything was taken care of that she needed for school and sports. In every sense of the word, I had become the parent of everyone in the house. As a teen, my relationship with my father eroded because I became resentful that so much responsibility was put on me. An alcoholic's illness isn't limited to them. It affects every single person they live with and every person who loves them.[12]

MOVIE BREAK: *WHEN A MAN LOVES A WOMAN*

In the movie, the mother, Alice (played by actress Meg Ryan), is an overdrinker. She has two daughters and a husband. One day Alice gets so drunk that she slaps her daughter and then loses her balance and has a bad fall. The daughter finds her mother lying unconscious on the floor and fears that she has died. She calls for help and it is decided that Alice indeed has a drinking problem. She is checked into rehab.[13]

LOSS OF SELF-ESTEEM

A parent's job is to lift their child up, help prepare them for the outside world, teach them by example to be a good person, and so much more along those same lines. Your overdrinking parent or parents are most likely not showing you a positive path to walk down. For some of you, your overdrinking parent could be doing more damage than good regarding raising you. Parents are supposed to help you see the worth in yourself and develop positive, healthy self-esteem as you grow up and get ready to venture out in to the world. That might be how it is working in your peers' non-overdrinking households, but you know better. In your parental overdrinking and dysfunctional household, your overdrinking parent might be the main person who hurts your self-esteem the most—more than any other bully at your school or stranger you come across out in public. That's not right and not how it is supposed to be. Your lack of self-esteem as a young adult that is caused by your overdrinking parent can also impact your self-esteem, or lack thereof, once you become an adult. Again, reversing the damage will take time, and the more support you can get to start healing, the better.

NARCISSISM

Narcissism is common for overdrinking parents. They can lose sight of what is truly important around them and just focus on their own needs and desires and what they think they deserve. It is all about them, not you, when in reality it is supposed to be about helping you, and not just concentrating on themselves. They think they are right all the time, and everyone else around them is wrong, even if you have proof and evidence. They think they are the most important person on the planet, and they will treat others like they are beneath them. They are on the proverbial high horse, and they think they are better and more important than everyone else.

MANIPULATION AND BRAINWASHING

Close to gaslighting, overdrinking parents will sometimes manipulate and brainwash others, especially you, their naive and innocent children. They will try to brainwash you and manipulate your decisions to try to sway them in a direction that benefits them— even if it puts the truth and your feelings at risk. They might start using you in ways that a parent should never treat their child. They know that you love them because you have a bond with them, and they will try to take advantage of that loving bond for their own personal and overdrinking gain.

WORRY AND FEAR

Living with an overdrinking parent can instill living in worry and fear. Since the household is constantly chaotic and dysfunctional and unpredictable, worry and fear can be present. You are constantly worried that your overdrinking parent will leave the stove on high while not in use with a towel next to it like Skeeter remembers. Or you feel fear or worry when your overdrinking parent walks through your front door, playing the guessing game of whether they are drunk or sober today. Worry and fear as a child can carry on later into your adulthood.

CHAPTER 11

Megan's Story

I have many terrible memories. What comes to mind first was when my mother left the house in her car and didn't return for two days. I couldn't sleep or eat and vomited multiple times, fearing the worst possible outcomes.

My mother's drinking affected my everyday life. When I was in elementary school, I worried that she would be late picking me up from school. When I was old enough to drive myself to and from school, I worried about the condition that mom would be in when I arrived at home. I worried whether my sister was safe when she returned home from school. I never really relaxed when I was out with my friends. I was worried about what was going on at home and if my little sister was safe.[14]

BLAME

This is a big one. Has your overdrinking parent ever blamed you for their drinking, especially when they were drunk? Or have you ever blamed yourself for your parent being an overdrinker? Remember that you are not to blame for your parent's overdrinking habits. You are not forcing a can of beer to their mouth every single night of the week. They are making that choice. You are not to blame—you never were, you never will be to blame, nor should you take any blame. Feeling like you are to blame all the time will make you feel like you are always doing something wrong. And then you start thinking that you always have to apologize, even if you aren't exactly sure what you need to apologize for. Then you start saying sorry about everything—even things that are not directly or indirectly linked to you at all. Don't do that to yourself, please. Be kind to yourself and realize this is just yet another psychological side effect of living with an overdrinking parent.

Megan's Story

No, my mother never said I caused her to drink. However, on my own, I had convinced myself that I caused her to drink because I mistakenly believed that if she loved her life as my mother, she wouldn't

118

want to drink. I felt she drank because she didn't enjoy her life and that she would be happier with a different kind of life. Every time I told her I felt this way, she cried. The truth is my mother has always loved my sister and me deeply but her addiction controlled her thoughts and behavior. Alcoholism ruled her. Her life became our life—one big, chaotic life that revolved around the destructive drinking. I longed to have my own life, but I couldn't imagine how I'd ever achieve that.

I became very anxious and always waiting for the next terrible thing to happen. I felt nervous all the time. I developed low self-esteem because I felt that I was somehow not good enough and that is why my mother drank. I know today that my mother's drinking had absolutely nothing to do with me and that she loves me very much. But when you're a kid, none of this is clear and the inconsistency in the love and affection that comes from an alcoholic makes it very difficult to believe that person when they are showering you with affection. I had a very normal reaction to the circumstances I faced. Today as an adult, I also have worked to overcome trust issues. My mother often let me down because of her addiction. I am always worried that people I love are going to let me down, even when they've done nothing to cause me to lose trust. I've worked hard on trusting my husband and my friends and family members and building healthy relationships with everyone around me.[15]

Veronica's Story
My father's drinking affected me in the ways I listed above. I suffered from depression, an anxiety disorder, panic attacks, which has since got better, but there are still difficulties that manifest in other areas of my life. I did not have any issues at school, rather, the situation with my family and my father led to an overcompensation of behavior in myself where I wanted to excel in school, and I always stayed on top of my studies. Regarding friends, I did not have many as I felt it hard to fit in. I always felt different, I was shy, inward, and also struggled with social anxiety in which my father's alcoholism and the effects no doubt contributed. I did have the occasional best friends and people I would

group myself with, but there was this constant, internal sense of not being able to be true to oneself; it was hard to be vulnerable (which I am a lot better with now and it can come easily) at that young of an age especially when it was hard to connect with others and "let loose" and enjoy things.[16]

Veronica's Story

I do not recall ever being blamed directly for it, but I do believe there may be an unconscious belief that formed that I was partially to blame. I never consciously felt or thought that it was my fault. My father would sometimes outlandishly blame my mother for some of his failures. I was so attached to my mother and unconsciously identified with her so in some way shape or form I probably did feel like I was responsible. Witnessing my father's drunken behaviors and how he would respond and behave to my mother, brother, and I contributed to me feeling like there was something inherently wrong with me, a feeling and internal experience that still is difficult to hold to this day.[17]

An annual average of 7.5 million children younger than the age of eighteen (10.5 percent of all children) live with a parent who has had an alcohol use disorder in the past year. These children are at a greater risk for depression, anxiety disorders, problems with cognitive and verbal skills, and parental abuse or neglect. Furthermore, they are four times more likely than other children to develop alcohol problems themselves.[18]

One in five adult Americans have lived with an alcoholic relative while growing up. In general, these children are at greater risk for having emotional problems than children whose parents are not alcoholics. Alcoholism runs in families, and children of alcoholics are four times more likely than other children to become alcoholics themselves. Most children of alcoholics have also experienced some form of neglect or abuse in the home.

A child being raised by a parent or caregiver who is suffering from alcohol abuse may have a variety of conflicting emotions that need to be addressed in order to avoid future problems. They are in a difficult position because they cannot go to their own parents for support. Some of the feelings can include the following:

- Guilt—The child may see himself or herself as the main cause of the mother's or father's drinking.

- Anxiety—The child may worry constantly about the situation at home. They may fear the alcoholic parent will become sick or injured and may also fear fights and violence between the parents.

- Embarrassment—Parents may give the child the message that there is a terrible secret at home. The ashamed child does not invite friends over and is afraid to ask anyone for help.

- Inability to have close relationships—Because the child has been disappointed by the drinking parent many times, trusting others becomes extremely difficult.

- Confusion—The alcoholic parent will suddenly change from being loving to angry, regardless of the child's behavior. A regular daily schedule, which is very important for a child, does not exist because bedtimes and mealtimes are constantly changing.

- Anger—The child feels anger at the alcoholic parent for drinking and may be angry at the nonalcoholic parent for lack of support and protection.

- Depression—The child feels lonely and helpless to change the situation.[19]

Overdrinking by a parent markedly increases health risks to children and adolescents. Such risks include diminished intellectual capacity and development, increased neuroticism, and a wide range of psychological and behavioral disorders. Parents who drink excessively are also likely to have children who experience long-term adverse consequences. These include heavy and problem-causing psychoactive substance use, criminality, suicide, depression, personality disorders, and psychological and behavioral disturbances. Parents who drink heavily are also especially likely to produce children who subsequently abstain from alcohol or drink only lightly.[20]

Although I know it is difficult, try to remember that dysfunction, chaos, and an overdrinking parental household leads to other psychological issues that can do more harm than good for you. Seeking out support, help, and less exposure to the overdrinking parent, especially when they are in their toxic overdrinking state, are key to getting through this and having less psychological harm done to you in the long run.

Part III

Resolution

Each of you will embark on a difficult journey, but it will be one that you don't have to walk alone. Trying to pave the way for your own future while trying to navigate an overdrinking parent at home will be no easy task. This book has given you tools, ideas, and perspectives from many others who have gone through and are going through what you are. If you will soon be able to distance yourself from the situation after you move away to college or you are about to rent your first apartment, getting space from your overdrinking parent will help you start your healing journey. Know that by moving ahead you will never have to go back to that situation ever again, unless you choose to. While growing up, you might not have had many other options to improve the situation at home. But now as you are getting older, you might have more control.

Healing is important for your mental well-being. Through time, some healing might even involve getting space from your overdrinking parent to readjust to your new life in a positive way, and to perhaps mend the bond with your overdrinking parent at a later date. Whether this may take months or years, only you will know through time. Each situation is different. Again, healing is healthy and getting distance away from your overdrinking parent is not you telling them you don't love them—it's you trying to heal from all the pain and stress to where you can become the best version of yourself. Parents want what is best for their children and their future, but an overdrinking parent can sometimes be blinded by their drinking and unable to see the clearer picture.

CHAPTER 12

The Healing Process

To heal is to learn how to give yourself what you need. For some of you, your overdrinking parent has left physical scars, while for others, your overdrinking parent has left you with more emotional, psychological scars. The scars may always remain, but as time pushes you forward in life, you can learn to forgive your overdrinking parent(s), heal yourself, and live your best life. The sooner you work on healing yourself, the sooner you won't be carrying your overdrinking parent's behavior and painful memories into your future relationships, to your future spouse, when you become a parent and raise children of your own. Please don't just bottle all this inside because that will cause problems for you later on in life. Tackle this head-on and address it right away. Join some support groups or start seeing a counselor, write in a diary or journal, or start exercising or going to church—take the time to heal yourself physically, emotionally, spiritually, mentally, and psychologically.

Healing is tricky if you are still under the same roof as your overdrinking parent. How do you heal when your parent is still overdrinking and adding new painful memories and stress to your life every day? At that point, I would say you are just surviving and trying to cope. To heal, really heal, on the inside and out, is a different process. Healing comes when you are no longer living under your overdrinking parent's roof anymore. Whether you leave home at eighteen and get your own place, move in with roommates, go off and join the army, leave and backpack through Europe, or get a job and move in with a relative—your healing won't begin until you are somehow removed or distanced from the situation involving your overdrinking parent. Healing takes time and is a process. Just by reading the participant stories from this book, you can see it doesn't happen overnight. You have to be patient.

It may take a few years of counseling sessions or support group sessions. You might need to make some changes to how you take care of your body such as joining yoga or getting regular massages, or increasing your willingness to trust by something like joining a church group and meeting new positive people—eventually be comfortable enough to open up to your teacher, coach, or someone you can trust to work through what happened. But just know that you can't really heal from an overdrinking parent until you are able to not be dealing with the overdrinking parent regularly.

Skeeter's Story

It took me a long time to realize what I had actually gone through. I was so busy working hard at school, playing sports, trying to find my own path in the world, that I was too distracted to realize that my childhood consisted of losing my mother young and then being raised by an overdrinking father. That was a lot on my plate as a kid and looking back I can't believe all that happened. It wasn't until recently when I realized I had been dealing with my overdrinking father's behavior longer than I have been grieving my late mother's death and was able to start my healing process. However, even though I am not living with my overdrinking father anymore and haven't for a while, he won't give me the space I need to truly start my healing process. For a few years he actually moved away to another state and that was the first time in my life I felt free from my rough past. During that time,

I took really great care of myself, I met a whole bunch of new people who are my dear friends to this day. I got support and went to counseling, and I just felt great and healthy and truly happy for once in my life. Those few years were amazing, and I felt like I finally became free—until my overdrinking father suddenly said he was moving back. I remember I almost had a panic attack over the phone when he said he was moving back to the state I lived in. When he moved away, I only had to deal with him via the phone. Dealing with him face-to-face and nearby is so much more stressful.[1]

Ava's Story

As an adult, I want nothing to do with alcohol or drugs. I have a sip every so often, but the thought and smell of alcohol make me sick to my stomach and drugs are even scarier. Even more so, everything that my mother did to me as a child has only made me want to do better for my own son. My mother is everything I don't want to be as a mom. I still struggle with everything she's put me through from time to time, but I have come a long way from where I was as a teenager when she first left my life. I give all the glory to God for where I'm at in the healing and coping.[2]

MOVIE BREAK: *SPIDER-MAN 3*

Separating the overdrinking from your parent is a difficult task. For all you superhero fans out there, think of how hard it was for Spider-Man to remove Venom from himself in the 2007 Tobey Maguire movie *Spider-Man 3*. Venom is a symbiote who clings to a suitable host. At first, Spider-Man likes how powerful he feels, but little does he know how fast Venom changes him in a not-so-good way. He realizes that he is starting to lose control of what Spider-Man truly stands for so long as Venom remains present and in control. Once he acknowledges that Venom does not represent his true self, Spider-Man has to gather all his willpower to take the Venom suit off. He successfully achieves this, but not without burning some bridges and needing some outside guidance in the process.[3]

Your parent liked how drinking initially made them feel—which led to them drinking even more. They can get help to stop overdrinking, but they are going to need some outside guidance to help them remove the temptation to chase that feeling. The longer they continue to drink and the more they drink, the more alcohol becomes like the new Venom symbiote for your parent. You still love your parent, the host underneath, but the longer the overdrinking happens, the more difficult detaching from alcohol is going to be. At this point they will need professional help in order to be able to do so.

Always remember no matter what harsh things are said or done—your parent whom you love, and who loves you, is still in there, but alcohol has become more in control of their brain than they are. I know that seems hard to accept, but try to focus on that aspect of all of this instead of each horrible thing that was said and done—that your parent is still in there somewhere. If you just focus on the bad and negative, that can complicate your healing process later. Try to let the good overpower the bad in this taxing situation.

Sometimes to heal, it is best not to keep rehashing bad memories of situations from over the years but, instead, to remember the good times. You may have more bad memories than good, but when it comes to healing, try to focus more on the good memories, as that will allow you to help cope and work through your negative memories.

Dilek's Story
As I said, my father was a fisherman. He used to go fishing whenever he had time. One day, he took me to the sea too. It was one of the best

days of my life because I was together with my daddy all day. I realized that I loved him so much and I never wanted him to drink even one glass. I realized that he was a good and loving daddy when he was not drunk.

We sailed, caught fish, ate lunch together. He showed me different kinds of fish. And I was the happiest in the world when we were back home! This was the most comforting day of my childhood.

I struggled with mental instability and depression during my bachelor years at the university. At some point, I learned that I could never change what happened in the past. I saw my father had changed after my brother was born. I can say that he completely stopped drinking. And he was very upset, sorry, and regretful for all these years. So, I said to myself that there was nothing to do except [forgiving] him and moving forward. I was very close to him five–six years before he died. We spent almost all these years talking about what happened in the past. Actually, he tried his best to make up for all the things he had done. And because I knew that his illness was worsening, I did my best to comfort him and persuade him that I forgave him and forgot all these bad memories.

I am [currently] a PhD student [abroad]. I am writing my dissertation on a project which I have been conducting since 2020 in the village where my father was born and grew up. As a result of this project, I am preparing a series of books which will document the tangible and intangible culture of the village. As a very important side product, I am writing my dissertation on this project using the autoethnography as my research method and reading a lot about autoethnography. It helps me heal because I know that I can heal if I go back to my memories and come to terms with them![4]

Sarah's Story

Once coming out of an extreme depressive episode, my mother took me out to the mall for the first time in years. I was seven years old. We went to Olga's Kitchen. I had missed her so much. I had spent the last seven months cutting her face out of family photos, banging and crying at her bedroom door to please let me in only to learn that she had escaped out her patio door to the neighbors down the street to drink. But in this moment, she was here with me. I remember her saying, "We should do this again sometime honey!" It felt good. I also remember coming home from some sort of camp as a child and my mom had redecorated my room. She bought me a cool green chair from Walmart and cleaned it for me. There was even a new comforter. I came home and felt so loved.

I have healed since the time I had to live with my mom. I try to remind myself that she was once just a very hurt, scared abused child herself. I learned more about her trauma and why she behaved the way she did. I truly try to treat her with kindness and forgive her for the past. I love reading books about the mother wound—it helps me learn why I developed OCD [obsessive-compulsive disorder] and how to cope with it now. I feel that I cope in positive ways. I talk to loved ones (my boyfriend and sister) when I struggle, I recently graduated from my therapy sessions. I love to ride my bike, be outside, cook and spend time with my animals.

[If I could tell my mother anything, I would say] Mom, I want you to know that I love you deeply. Your struggles with alcohol do not define the person you are. I want you to know that I forgive you for everything. I understand that your past was incredibly difficult, and you never had the chance to heal from it. We're all just navigating this complex world together.[5]

Skeeter's Story

My dad knew how much I loved to ride my bike. Looking back now, I have ridden my bike a lot in my life. I think it has been a way for me to cope with everything life has thrown at me. One day, my dad was sober, and he said he wanted to take a father–daughter bike-riding trip. It was after my mother passed away. We ended up riding ten miles and saw so many beautiful parts of the city we lived in. We stopped to rest and grabbed lunch and even some ice cream. We were so sore when we finished our ride and came home, but spending time with my father, sober, after everything that had happened, made me feel like for just that one day, he chose me over the bottle. And I felt loved.[6]

Megan's Story

My mother has an alcohol use disorder. Yes, she still suffers from it to this day. However, I'm grateful to share that despite still being an active alcoholic, my mother is doing significantly better today. Her addiction does not have the same control over her as it once did, and she is living in healthier ways. Our relationship is better than I ever dreamed it would be, thanks to her improvements and because I worked hard on my own healing. I set and stuck to boundaries with my mother. I focused on myself, got educated and healed from those experiences. When one person in a family gets healthier, everyone in the family benefits from it, including the person with the substance use disorder.

My mother and I share a similar sense of humor. When I was in high school, I recall watching an episode of the comedy show Saturday Night Live *with my father and mother. There was a skit that my mother and I thought was hilarious. We laughed until tears ran down our cheeks and so hard that my stomach muscles burned. There is no greater joy for me than seeing my mother sober and happy.*

Today, I am so thrilled to share that I am living a life I love. Over the last fifteen years, I have been focused on my healing. It has taken quite a bit of courage and time to heal from everything that happened in the past. I continue to see a therapist, read personal growth books, listen to well-being health podcasts, and connect with other people who have loved ones who are active or recovered alcoholics. It is truly a lifelong journey, and it so more than worth it.

I'm a firm believer that healing is not only possible, but it happens much faster than one would imagine. I've made so much progress I can barely recognize the person I was at twenty-six years old when I started my healing journey. I have responded in very positive ways to focusing on my healing. Sometimes, I fall backward and revert into my old ways of thinking and living. When that happens, I must double down on my self-care activities and focus on continuing my healing.

For me, the most powerful step in my healing journey as an adult child of an alcoholic was understanding the science of addiction. It's clear that people who develop substance use disorders are usually wonderful, kind, and smart people. My mother is an exceptionally compassionate and kind person who has a flair for home decorating and making people feel special. Tragically, she developed a substance use disorder very early in life and that affected her roles as a mother and wife. Her body became dependent on alcohol to function, and over time, the alcohol affected her brain. It controls her thoughts and actions. Just as cancer and other diseases take over a body, addiction does the same. Addiction makes people do terrible things.

It took me many years to understand that my mother's substance use disorder had nothing to do with me, my sister, or my father and, despite all my efforts, I had zero control over my mother or her substance use disorder. The only way to escape addiction is to get professional help. Some can successfully do this; some try and fail. Others never try at all. People who love people with substance use disorders cannot control any of this; all we can do is recognize those loved ones for the good people they are, despite their disorder. For me, I recognize and celebrate the many good qualities my mother has and for the mother she would have been if she never developed a substance use disorder.[7]

Healing is also remembering the happy memories. The more happy memories you can remember, the more they can start replacing the negative ones over time.

Veronica's Story

I am currently in therapy, and it has and continues to work wonders. I have worked with traditional talk therapies that have given me so much insight but work with the body is just as important, as emotions reside there too. As a teenager, although I did not engage in any external behaviors that would have harmed me more, I did spend a lot of time using escapism as a coping mechanism. Old Hollywood films, vintage films in general, and the collecting of books was what helped me as it offered me so much. The time spent with old films and their respective decades eventually led me to study the topic in university, and now in graduate school. I also read a lot of about psychology/psychoanalysis, which helped me to realize that cinema for me was a place to meet myself through different stories, archetypes, characters, and situations. Cinema has been one of the greatest healing tools for me alongside therapy.[8]

JODY LAMB'S EXPERT INSIGHT REGARDING THE HEALING PROCESS

Jody Lamb, author, speaker, and advocate, shares her expert insight when it comes to teenagers taking healing steps.

The first step of the healing process from all of this is to first recognize that you had a normal response to your situation. The good news is this step is probably happening right now as you read this book. If you realize that your parent's overdrinking affected you, the next step is to go all in on taking good care of yourself. The most impactful way to do that is surrounding yourself with all the positive people and activities that will help you set your path forward and remind you that the difficult times you're experiencing now will pass. You are an independent person with the power to create a life you love and deserve in the future.

I've come across thousands of people who grew up with a parent who overdrinks. Today, they are enjoying a completely different life than they did when they were all wrapped up in the chaos surrounded by their parent's overdrinking. Fortunately, they were able to get educated about substance use like you are doing and healed from their experiences.

The people who are physically near you may not have the same level of hope and determination to have a different life than you do. That's why it's important to find more positive voices in other ways. Listen to podcasts and social media content from people who inspire you. Make sure the majority of words you hear every day are positive. Ignore the negative, hurtful, and destructive words of others who may be around you. Listen to music that makes you feel good. Try new things and be open to things that other people find to be helpful for their well-being. This could be taking on a new sport or creative outlet. I picked up creative writing as a hobby, and through it, I made new friends who encouraged and inspired me. Their voices helped silence the Negative Nellies around me.

Canadian Olympian runner Leah Pells found peace and serenity as a young person through running. It was her way of coping with the chaos caused by her mother's overdrinking. When she was running, Leah explained in her memoir, Not About the Medal, *all her worries about her mother's drinking went away. Perhaps through running, she was Leah the runner, not Leah, the daughter of the lady who overdrinks. Find something that feels freeing and give time to it, even if you only have fifteen minutes per day for it.*[9]

FORGIVE YOURSELF

Forgive yourself for accidentally enabling your overdrinking parent. Forgive yourself for thinking stressful thoughts or maybe losing patience. Forgive yourself for not knowing how to handle your parent's behavior. Remember that you are your overdrinking parent's child, and it's not a normal everyday situation to try and figure out. Your peers aren't having to deal with that, so forgive yourself for not knowing how to handle the situation perfectly. Not every teenager or young adult has to live through this situation, so just forgive yourself for being innocent and for not really knowing how to navigate it all. It's okay. You did not do anything wrong.

LEARNING TO FORGIVE YOUR OVERDRINKING PARENT

This can be extremely challenging, and it might take a while to reach the point when you're ready to even consider this. If abuse is still happening in the now, and you are still being exposed to your overdrinking parent's behavior and still might even be living under their roof, chances are forgiveness is not on your radar as of yet. Maybe you moved out a couple of years ago and the time apart and distance have helped you heal where you are almost ready to forgive them. Or maybe it has been several years that you have been able to self-reflect on the whole situation, and maybe your parent made the first move and sincerely apologized to you first. Maybe you are at the point where you are ready to forgive them. Each journey is different. Your healing journey from your overdrinking parent will be different than even your sibling's healing journey from the same overdrinking parent. So understand that when you are ready to forgive, if you will ever be ready to forgive, then you will do it on your own terms. It may be now, or later, or after your overdrinking parent passes away. Only you know when and if that time will ever come. Forgiveness can be a positive healing milestone for you, and it is better to forgive than to stay angry and bitter and bottle everything up for your whole life—but again that is a decision only you can make.

Skeeter's Story

I have noticed that, looking back now, I beat myself up a lot for everything that happened. Maybe if I realized I was enabling him all those years and stopped picking him up at the bars, that maybe he would have stopped drinking years ago and we could have had a better relationship. I know that type of magical thinking is just mere daydreaming, but I beat myself up a lot. Maybe I should have been more patient or understanding or less judging all of these years as to why he drinks so much.

I love my father. I always have and always will. I don't hate him. I am not mad at him. I forgive him. I am sorry for how I may have hurt him over the years too. I just wish things were different. I am sad to think of how many happy memories we missed out on. I wish he got help and counseling for his overdrinking years ago. I am not sharing all of this to hurt him. In many ways I am sharing all of this because I love him. I hope we still have time to fix this.[10]

Georgianne's Story
When I was young, I was so angry at my overdrinking mother. I would tell her that she was selfish and did not care about us. I would tell her that I am sorry you were not strong enough to deal with what life presented you and that you did not get help for your problem.

However, now as a Christian adult woman, I have forgiven her time after time and hope she is at peace.[11]

CHAPTER 13

Sins of the Overdrinking Parent Do Not Have to Mean Sins for You

"Alcoholism tends to run in families: compared with children of non-alcoholics (non-COAs), children of alcoholic parents (COAs) have an approximately four times greater risk of becoming alcoholic themselves."[1] Just because your parent overdrinks doesn't mean you have to as well. You always have a choice. No one will force you to drink something. Yes, genetics can play a part in overdrinking throughout generations, but can anyone technically force anyone to put a drink to their mouth? Some struggle with alcohol addiction, but they are still making a choice to drink something specific. No one is forcing anyone to choose beer over water. Yes, the chances are higher if there's an overdrinking parent for a child to grow up to be an overdrinker as well, but there could also be extenuating circumstances. Children learn certain behaviors from their parents. If their overdrinking parent shows their overdrinking behavior to their children, children can grow up mirroring that behavior. But that doesn't mean that every single child who has an overdrinking parent will become an overdrinker themselves one day. Some children will grow up and know that their parent's overdrinking behavior is not healthy and will course-correct their life to stay on a non-overdrinking path because they witnessed firsthand what happens when someone walks down an overdrinking path. And don't be scared thinking that because your parent overdrinks that you will automatically become an overdrinker when you get older as well, because that is simply not true. There's a chance you could, but you have the power to say no. You can take steps right now to make sure you don't follow the same overdrinking path your overdrinking parent walked down. You can make good choices and know to hang out with non-overdrinking friends. You can skip the whole partying stage at twenty-one and not make finally being of age to drink a big deal. You can limit yourself when you do reach drinking age and make sure you stay in control and aren't easily influenced by peer pressure. You can go to counseling and arm yourself with anti-overdrinking skills to fight the urge if it comes and if you want to avoid this stage. You have the willpower to simply say, "No thank you." If someone offers you a drink, you have the willpower to control what you drink and put in your body. If you need further deterrence, create a family and friend group that can help you stay on a positive non-overdrinking path. Having support from those who love you can help you if you're struggling to avoid walking down a path of overdrinking.

Skeeter's Story

Growing up, I was always spending time with my mother while my brother was always spending time with my father. They would do guy things, and my mom and I would do girly things. They would go on guys' trips, invite a group of guys over to watch football or a boxing match. My mom and I would go shopping, or paint our nails, or visit family and friends out and about. Since my father is the overdrinker, my brother got way more exposed to his drinking than I did. However, I started getting exposed after my mother died. Then it was just my brother, my father, and me. I always remember feeling like the third wheel around them. My dad would take my brother shopping but then would ask family or friends who were girls to take me shopping. I never went on the father son trips after my mother died. But I remember that life changed so much after my mom died. I was aware before she died that my father overdrank, but looking back I think my mom protected me from getting exposed for the most part to my dad's overdrinking. I consciously made a choice when I was younger to never drink alcohol in my life. Years have gone by, and I even skipped the whole drinking at twenty-one years old stage with my peers. I never partied and I never gave into peer pressure. My brother was exposed to my father's overdrinking his whole childhood. He is now an overdrinker himself. It has been difficult to watch all these years, because I feel like he never would have traveled down this path of overdrinking had my father not been his father. Looking back, overdrinking has ruined their lives. I have seen it affect their relationships, their marriages, their bank accounts, their children, and even diminish their hopes and dreams. My father was exposed to his father's overdrinking before him and now my brother was exposed to my father's overdrinking. It is a terrible cycle that has affected generations of my family.[2]

"Although many factors influence substance misuse, research shows that children of parents with an AUD (alcohol use disorder) are more likely to engage in alcohol or substance misuse themselves."[3]

You have a choice to eat healthy food or unhealthy food; drink water or beer; go to sleep early or go to sleep late; and spend money on this or that—you will have to make decisions every day for the rest of your life and you have to live with your decisions and their consequences. Use your parent's overdrinking behavior as an example—Do you want to end up exactly like your parent? If you use their life as a reference for how you want to live or not want to live, then you have a chance to not make the same mistakes they made, especially pertaining to overdrinking behavior. You decide which road you want to take. Your sober parent and overdrinking parent cannot tell you which path to choose nor force you one way or the other. You are responsible for the decisions you make.

CHAPTER 14

Parting Advice

IT'S ALWAYS EASY TO THINK THAT IN A DIFFICULT MOMENT YOU are the only one on the planet who has ever gone through something hard. It makes sense to think that way, because unless you know someone in your close circle who went through a situation, or is currently going through a situation, how do you know there are really thousands or even millions more people on Earth who have also navigated this as well? My hopes for you, dear reader, after reading this book, is that you have learned that you are not alone in this. Between the facts and statistics and stories of other participants from this book alone, you can see you are not the only one who is going through this.

As a farewell from reading this book, those who participated wanted to send you off with some final thoughts that can help you navigate your own overdrinking parental situation. They all have navigated an overdrinking parent before you and wanted to share some advice that can help you gain some perspective into your own situation.

Dilek

Understanding the reason behind a problem is the most important key! And forgiving is the best possible and doable way to free yourself and your alcoholic parent! The physical abuse can be forgotten easily, but the mental abuse cannot be forgotten but can be forgiven if you love your parent truly and if you can understand what happened around their life.[1]

Georgianne

My advice to the young children of today is that there is all kinds of help out there now. [Long ago], when there was nothing and everything was kept quiet, things were just swept under the rug, as they say. You should not have to suffer through your parents' addiction. You are not responsible for them or for their problems. You shouldn't have to act as the adult in the house. Find help, continue to get help as long as it takes for you to have a good and happy life because life is short and not fair but you can try to make yours better.[2]

Ava

You are not your parents. You may look like them, but you are not them. You are your own individual human being with a unique purpose and calling in life. Don't let your parents define who you are. If a friend invites you to church, take them up on it. God is real. Jesus Christ is real, and He is waiting on you. Life is so much better when you finally receive that peace that only God can give you. Find a trusting adult to confide in. Talk about how you feel and if you're in danger, tell someone immediately.[3]

Megan

Life right now is temporary. It is going to get better in the future. The life you have now will look very different than the one that you can have in the future as an adult. I have met thousands of people who've grown up with overdrinking parents like you who are now healthy and happy people living the lives they want. It can be difficult to imagine feeling different than you do today, but you can dramatically change your life in the future.

It is not your fault that your parent is addicted to alcohol. Substance use disorders are brain disorders. You cannot cause someone to drink or to become addicted to alcohol.

You cannot control or cure or fix an overdrinker. They must want to accept help on their own. It is not your job to fix your parent. It is their job to take good care of themselves and to get help to overcome their disorder.

Your only job in life is to take good care of yourself. It is not your job to take care of your parents or your siblings. Always put yourself first. Focus on your own education about addiction and what's happening to your parents. Take advantage of opportunities for talking to a counselor at school or a therapist. Seek out information online such as through Alateen to connect with other kids who are growing up in a similar type of environment. The healthier you are, the healthier your siblings and your parents will be.

Separate the addiction from the person your parent is at heart. This is an extremely difficult thing to do when you're living with an active overdrinker. But a substance use disorder is a medical condition that requires medical treatment. Your parent must want to accept help to get better. Let your parent know that you love them and the qualities you appreciate in them. Let them know that you will support them when they seek help. But do not obsess or get preoccupied with convincing them to get help. It is their journey to make, not yours. Recognize the good in them.[4]

Sarah

You might feel stuck right now, but it is not your forever. Your overdrinking parent does NOT define you, in any way, shape or form. One day this will be part of your story, and you will share it with others who are fighting this battle too. You will learn exactly who you do not want to be in life and the challenges you faced as a child, will prepare you to climb any mountain in life. Focus on school, being outside, immerse yourself in books and hobbies to pass time. Do not be scared to reach out for help. No one will pity you; they will admire you for your bravery. One day this will pass, and you will be free, I promise.[5]

Skeeter

Remember that living with your overdrinking parent is not permanent. Whether you move away to college once you turn eighteen, or your aunt will let you live with her at sixteen, or wherever life takes you, you won't be feeling stressed out and stuck for the rest of your life. Healing is a process, but a healthy way to cope with the situation you were innocently put in. No kid wants to be born to parents who overdrink. We love our parents, and it makes us sad that they went down this path and we were affected, but this situation does not have to define your life nor block you from having the happy life you truly desire and deserve. Whether your parent stops drinking one day is entirely up to them and is out of your control. You shouldn't worry about any of that. You need to focus on how to heal yourself so you can have a more positive future although your past has been quite difficult perhaps this far. You didn't cause your parent to overdrink so don't ever blame yourself. You do not have to walk down your overdrinking parents' path. You have the power to choose your own path. Learn from your overdrinking parent's mistakes. Don't hold on to anger. Forgive them. Love them still—but there is nothing wrong with getting healthy distance from them if they are causing negativity in your life. You only get to live one life. Life is very short and very fast. Enjoy every second of it, and don't let this difficult moment hinder you from having a happy and healthy life.[6]

Veronica

You have so much mental and emotional resilience in you even though you may not believe it or it does not seem like it. No matter what gets hurled at you, what you have to endure, do not extinguish that part of you, that spark, that calls to you to remain and to hold on; you are here for a reason and your feelings and experiences matter and are seen; your parents' drinking is not your fault. Although it may be hard to do, reach out to someone that you trust to talk about what you are experiencing or seek out support groups—I do not think you will regret it!

The Swiss psychoanalyst Carl Jung had said that "God enters through the wound." Whether or not you are deeply religious, or spiritual, I think that this is a beautiful quote to describe that despite our personal suffering, our difficulties are not devoid of meaning but rather illustrate the transformative powers of pain. Yes, the wounding is painful, but the wound could also be looked at as a transformative entryway where we can come to gain knowledge about ourselves and a deeper connection, if willing, to a higher power or even with the energies of the world around us. Wounding is integral to the human condition and in this we are not alone.[7]

Hang in there. It's not easy, but you *will* get through this.

Helpful Resources

Books
7 Things That Change Everything by Jody Lamb
The ACOA Trauma Sydnrome: The Impact of Childhood Trauma on Adult Relationships by Dr. Tian Dayton
Adult Children of Alcoholics by Dr. Janet G. Woititz, EdD
Adult Children of Alcoholics/Dysfunctional Families (The Big Red Book) by ACA (Adult Children of Alcoholics)
After the Tears: Helping Adult Children of Alcoholics Heal Their Childhood Trauma by Jane Middleton-Moz and Lorie Dwinell
The Body Keeps the Score: Brain, Mind, and Body in the Healing of Trauma by Bessel van der Kolk, MD
Codependence and the Power of Detachment: How to Set Boundaries and Make Your Life Your Own by Karen Casey
Codependent No More by Melody Beattie
Courage to Change—One Day at a Time (Al-Anon)
Dear Kids of Alcoholics by Lindsey Hall and Leigh Cohn
Easter Ann Peters's Operation Cool by Jody Lamb
"It Will Never Happen to Me!" Children of Alcoholics: As Youngsters-Adolescents-Adults by Claudia Black, PhD
Love First: A Family's Guide to Intervention by Jeff and Debra Jay
Not about the Medal by Leah Pells
One Day at a Time (Al-Anon)
Perfect Daughters: Adult Daughters of Alcoholics by Robert Ackerman, PhD
Playing It by Heart: Taking Care of Yourself No Matter What by Melody Beattie
There Was a. Little Girl: The Real Story of My Mother and Me by Brooke Shields

Hotline Numbers
Child Help National Child Abuse Hotline: (800) 422–4453
National Domestic Violence Hotline: (800) 799–7233
National Sexual Assault Hotline: (800) 656–4673

National Suicide and Crisis Lifeline: 988
Substance Abuse and Mental Health Services Administration: 1–800–662–HELP (4357)

PODCASTS

"Adult Children of Alcoholics with Dr. Claudia Black," episode 134 of *Soberful* by Veronica Valli and Chip Somers, https://podcasts.apple.com/us/podcast/adult-children-of-alcoholics-with-dr-claudia-black/id1371013717?i=1000515161045.

"Helping Adult Children of Alcoholics," Season 3, episode 6, of *Beyond Theory* with Dr. Tian Dayton, https://beyondtheorypodcast.com/dr-tian-dayton-helping-adult children-of-alcoholics/.

Sarah and Amy: The Children of Alcoholics Podcast, https://hello9a.podbean.com/.

"Understanding Adult Children of Alcoholics or Addicts: ACOA with Jody Lamb," episode 540 of *The Chalene Show*, with Chalene Jobson, https://chalene.com/podcasts/adult-children-alcoholics-lamb/.

Voices Across America: Sharing Stories of Living with Alcoholics. https://podcasts.apple.com/us/podcast/aca-adult-children-voices-across-america-speaker-meeting/id1592765405.

WEBSITES

Adult Children of Alcoholics and Dysfunctional Families World Service Organization. https://adultchildren.org/.

Al-Anon Family Groups. https://al-anon.org/.

Alateen. https://al-anon.org/for-members/group-resources/alateen/.

Alcoholics Anonymous. https://www.aa.org/.

American Academy of Child and Adolescent Psychiatry. https://www.aacap.org/aacap/Families_and_Youth/Facts_for_Families/FFF-Guide/Children-Of-Alcoholics-17.aspx.

American Addiction Centers. https://americanaddictioncenters.org/blog/10-traits-of-adult-children-of-alcoholics.

American Psychological Association. Hotlines, Resources, and to Seek Counseling in Your State. https://www.apa.org/topics/crisis-hotlines.

Better Help. https://www.betterhelp.com/advice/teenagers/how-to-cope-with-alcoholic-parents/.

Eluna Network. Camp Mariposa. https://elunanetwork.org/camps-programs/camp-mariposa

Hazelden Betty Ford Foundation. https://www.hazeldenbettyford.org/articles/adult-children-of-alcoholics.

Jody Lamb. Children of Alcoholics Influencer. https://www.jodylamb.com/.

Kids Health/Teens Health. https://kidshealth.org/en/teens/coping-alcoholic.html.

Mental Health America. https://www.mhanational.org/co-dependency.
National Association for Children of Addiction. https://nacoa.org/
Nacoa UK. https://nacoa.org.uk/
National Institute on Alcohol Abuse and Alcoholism. https://www.niaaa.nih
.gov/our-work/donations-niaaa.
Substance Abuse and Mental Health Services Administration. https://www
.samhsa.gov/find-help/national-helpline.

Notes

Part I

1. "Alcohol's Effects on Health," National Institute on Alcohol Abuse and Alcoholism, updated 2024, https://www.niaaa.nih.gov/alcohol -health/overview-alcohol-consumption/moderate-binge-drinking#:~:text =According%20to%20the, accessed May 7, 2024.
2. Ibid.
3. Ibid.
4. The Editors of *Encyclopedia Britannica*, "Alcoholic Beverage," *Encyclopedia Britannica*, last updated July 15, 2024, https://www.britannica .com/topic/alcoholic-beverage, accessed May 7, 2024.

Chapter 1

1. Rachel N. Lipari and Struther L. Van Horn, *The CBHSQ Report: Children Living with Parents Who Have a Substance Use Disorder*. Center for Behavioral Health Statistics and Quality (CBHDQ), August 24, 2024, https://www.samhsa.gov/data/sites/default/files/report_3223/ShortReport -3223.html, accessed February 1, 2024.
2. Skeeter, email interview, May 7, 2024.
3. Dilek, email interview, December 11, 2022.
4. Georgianne, email interview, May 6, 2024.
5. Sarah, email interview, May 19, 2024.
6. Megan, email interview, February 4, 2024.
7. *Flight*. Drama. Thriller. 2012. 138 minutes.
8. *Hacksaw Ridge*. Biography. Drama. History. 2016. 139 minutes.

Chapter 2

1. Erin L. George, "What Happens to Children of Alcoholic Parents?" MentalHelp.net, https://www.mentalhelp.net/parenting/what-happens-to -children-of-alcoholic-parents/, accessed February 1, 2024.

2. Skeeter, email interview, May 7, 2024.
3. Ava, email interview, May 8, 2024.
4. Dilek, email interview, December 11, 2022.
5. Georgianne, email interview, May 6, 2024.
6. Sarah, email interview, May 19, 2024.
7. Megan, email interview, February 4, 2024.
8. Skeeter, email interview, May 7, 2024.
9. Veronica, email interview, May 23, 2024.

CHAPTER 3
1. Skeeter, email interview, May 7, 2024.
2. Sarah, email interview, May 19, 2024.
3. Megan, email interview, February 4, 2024.
4. Colin McEvoy, "Jamie Lee Curtis," *Biography*, last updated March 29, 2024, https://www.biography.com/actors/jamie-lee-curtis#inbox/_blank, accessed February 19, 2024.
5. "Tony Curtis," Biography.com, https://www.biography.com/actors/tony-curtis, accessed February 19, 2024.
6. Dorany Pineda, "Ben Affleck Opens Up About Alcohol Addiction, Depression and His Biggest Disappointment," *Los Angeles Times*, February 20, 2020, https://www.latimes.com/entertainment-arts/movies/story/2020-02-20/ben-affleck-alcohol-addiction-depression-disappointment#inbox/_blank, accessed April 7, 2024.
7. Claudia Harmata, "Carol Burnett's Tragic History with Addiction in the Family: 'You Can't Cure Them,'" *People*, August 20, 2020, https://people.com/tv/carol-burnett-history-with-addiction-in-the-family/, accessed April 7th 2024.
8. Alexia Fernández, "Demi Moore Says Her 'Addiction' to Ashton Kutcher Was 'Devastating': 'It Took Me Away Emotionally,'" *People*, November 4, 2019, https://people.com/movies/demi-moore-addiction-ashton-kutcher-was-devastating/#inbox/_blank, accessed May 29, 2024.
9. Tim Teeman, "Like Father Like Son," *Irish Examiner*, June 16, 2012, https://www.irishexaminer.com/lifestyle/celebrity/arid-20197561.html#inbox/_blank, accessed April 7, 2024.
10. Micheal Tauber, "How Robin Williams Fought, and Lost, His Battles with Addiction and Depression," *People*, August 13, 2014, https://people.com/celebrity/how-robin-williams-fought-and-lost-his-battles-with-addiction-and-depression/, accessed May 7, 2024.
11. "Eugene O'Neill," Nobel Prize.org, https://www.nobelprize.org/prizes/literature/1936/oneill/facts/, accessed February 19, 2024.

12. Jim Gigliotti, *Who Was Ernest Hemingway?* (New York: Penguin Random House, 2022).
13. Veronica, email interview, May 23, 2024
14. "Children: The Silent Victims of Parental Alcoholism and Substance Use," Brook Lane.org, https://www.brooklane.org/blog/children-silent-victims-parental-alcoholism-substance-use, accessed February 1, 2024.

CHAPTER 4

1. *The Butterfly Effect.* Drama. Sci-Fi. Thriller. 2004. 113 minutes.
2. *Forrest Gump.* Drama. Romance. 1994. 142 minutes.
3. *The Shack.* Drama. Fantasy. 2017. 132 minutes.
4. *I Can Only Imagine.* Biography. Drama. Family. 2018. 110 minutes.
5. Dilek, email interview, December 11, 2022.
6. Georgianne, email interview, May 6, 2024.
7. Skeeter, email interview, May 7, 2024.
8. Sarah, email interview, May 19, 2024.
9. Veronica, email interview, May 23, 2024.
10. "Take the ACEs Quiz," American Society for the Positive Care of Children, https://americanspcc.org/take-the-aces-quiz/, accessed May 24, 2024.
11. Ibid.
12. Lizmarie Maldonado, "Alcoholism Statistics and Important Facts," American Addiction Center ProjectKnow.com, last updated November 1, 2023, https://projectknow.com/alcohol/statistics/, accessed February 1, 2024.

CHAPTER 5

1. "Overview of Alcohol Consumption," National Institute on Alcohol Abuse and Alcoholism, https://www.niaaa.nih.gov/alcohols-effects-health/overview-alcohol-consumption, accessed May 8, 2024.
2. "Understanding Alcohol Use Disorder," National Institute on Alcohol Abuse and Alcoholism, last updated July 2024, https://www.niaaa.nih.gov/publications/brochures-and-fact-sheets/understanding-alcohol-use-disorder, accessed May 8, 2024.
3. "Alcohol and the Brain: An Overview," National Institute on Alcohol Abuse and Alcoholism, published 2022, https://www.niaaa.nih.gov/publications/alcohol-and-brain-overview, accessed May 9, 2024.
4. "Drinking Too Much Alcohol Can Harm Your Health," Centers for Disease Control and Prevention, https://www.cdc.gov/alcohol/fact-sheets/alcohol-use.htm, accessed May 9, 2024.
5. Dilek, email interview, December 11, 2022.
6. Jody Lamb, email interview, May 19, 2024.

Chapter 6

1. "Biology of Addiction: Drugs and Alcohol Can Hijack Your Brain," *News in Health*, October 2015, https://newsinhealth.nih.gov/2015/10/biology-addiction, accessed May 29, 2024.
2. Ava, email interview, May 8, 2024.
3. Georgianne, email interview, May 6, 2024.
4. Megan, email interview, February 4, 2024.
5. Skeeter, email interview, May 7, 2024.
6. Jody Lamb, email interview, May 19, 2024.

Chapter 7

1. *Saving Mr. Banks*. 2013. 125 minutes.
2. Raechal Shewfelt, "As Colin Farrell Returns to Rehab, We Look Back at What He's Said about Addiction," *Yahoo Entertainment*, April 4, 2018, https://www.yahoo.com/entertainment/colin-farrell-returns-rehab-look-back-hes-said-addiction-224134118.html, accessed May 30, 2024.
3. Georgianne, email interview.
4. Skeeter, email interview, May 7, 2024.
5. Ibid.

Chapter 8

1. Skeeter, email interview, May 7, 2024.
2. Ava, email interview, May 8, 2024.
3. Dilek, email interview, December 11, 2022.
4. Sarah, email interview, May 19, 2024.
5. Megan, email interview, February 4, 2024.
6. Veronica, email interview, May 23, 2024.

Chapter 9

1. Georgianne, email interview, May 6, 2024.
2. Sarah, email interview, May 19, 2024.
3. Skeeter, email interview, May 7, 2024.
4. Ava, email interview, May 8, 2024.
5. Ibid.

Chapter 10

1. Megan, email interview, February 4, 2024.
2. Veronica, email interview, May 23, 2024.
3. Megan, email interview, February 4, 2024.
4. Veronica, email interview, May 23, 2024.

Chapter 11

1. Skeeter, email interview, May 7, 2024.
2. Megan, email interview, February 4, 2024.
3. Jody Lamb, email interview, May 19, 2024.
4. Skeeter, email interview, May 7, 2024.
5. Ava, email interview, May 8, 2024.
6. *Renfield*. 2023. Horror. Comedy. 93 minutes.
7. Skeeter, email interview, May 7, 2024.
8. Sarah, email interview, May 19, 2024.
9. *Angela's Ashes*. Biography. Drama. 1999. 145 minutes.
10. Skeeter, email interview, May 7, 2024.
11. Veronica, email interview, May 23, 2024.
12. Megan, email interview, February 4, 2024.
13. *When a Man Loves a Woman*. Drama. Romance. 1994. 126 minutes.
14. Ibid.
15. Ibid.
16. Veronica, email interview, May 23, 2024.
17. Ibid.
18. "More than 7 Million Children Live with a Parent with Alcohol Problems," *Data Spotlight*, February 16, 2012, Center for Behavioral Health Statistics and Quality, https://www.samhsa.gov/data/sites/default/files/Spot061ChildrenOfAlcoholics2012/Spot061ChildrenOfAlcoholics2012.pdf, accessed February 1, 2024.
19. Ibid.
20. M. A. Plant, J. Orford, and M. Grant, "The Effects on Children and Adolescents of Parents' Excessive Drinking: An International Review," *Public Health Report* 104, no. 5 (1989): 433–42, https://www.ncbi.nlm.nih.gov/pmc/articles/PMC1579958/#:~:text=Parents%20who%20drink%20excessively%20are,and%20psychological%20and%20behavioral%20disturbances, accessed August 6, 2024.

Chapter 12

1. Skeeter, email interview, May 7, 2024.
2. Ava, email interview, May 8, 2024.
3. *Spider-Man 3*. Action. Adventure. Sci-Fi. 2007. 139 minutes.
4. Dilek, email interview, December 11, 2022.
5. Sarah, email interview, May 19, 2024.
6. Skeeter, email interview, May 7, 2024.
7. Megan, email interview, February 4, 2024.
8. Veronica, email interview, May 23, 2024.
9. Jody Lamb, email interview, May 19, 2024.

10. Skeeter, email interview, May 7, 2024.
11. Georgianne, email interview, May 6, 2024.

Chapter 13

1. Wendy Reich, "Prospective Studies of Children of Alcoholic Parents," *Alcohol Health Research World* 21, no. 3 (1997): 255–57, https://www.ncbi.nlm.nih.gov/pmc/articles/PMC6826816/#:~:text=Alcoholism%20tends%20to%20run%20in,Cotton%201979%3B%20Merikangas%20et%20al, accessed February 1, 2024.
2. Skeeter, email interview, May 7, 2024.
3. Stacy Mosel, "Children of Alcoholics: Growing up with an Alcoholic Parent," American Addiction Centers, last updated June 18, 2024, https://americanaddictioncenters.org/alcohol/support-recovery/child, accessed February 1, 2024.

Chapter 14

1. Dilek, email interview, December 11, 2022.
2. Georgianne, email interview, May 6, 2024.
3. Ava, email interview, May 8, 2024.
4. Megan, email interview, February 4, 2024.
5. Sarah, email interview, May 19, 2024.
6. Skeeter, email interview, May 7, 2024.
7. Veronica, email interview, May 23, 2024.

Bibliography

"Alcohol and the Brain: An Overview." National Institute on Alcohol Abuse and Alcoholism. https://www.niaaa.nih.gov/publicataions/alcohol-and -brain-overview. Accessed May 8, 2024.

"Alcohol Use in Families." American Academy of Child and Adolescent Psychiatry, last updated May 2019. https://www.aacap.org/AACAP /Families_and_Youth/Facts_for_Families/FFF-Guide/Children-Of -Alcoholics-017.aspx. Accessed February1, 2024.

"Alcohol's Effects on Health." National Institute on Alcohol Abuse and Alcoholism, last updated 2024. https://www.niaaa.nih.gov/alcohol -health/overview-alcohol-consumption/moderate-binge-drinking#:~:text =According%20to%20the. Accessed May 7, 2024.

"Alcoholism Statistics and Important Facts." American Addiction Center ProjectKnow.com. https://projectknow.com/alcohol/statistics/. Accessed February 1, 2024.

"Biology of Addiction: Drugs and Alcohol Can Hijack Your Brain." *News in Health,* October 2015. https://newsinhealth.nih.gov/2015/10/biology -addiction. Accessed May 29, 2024.

Britannica, the Editors of Encyclopaedia. "alcoholic beverage." *Encyclopedia Britannica,* last updated July 15, 2024. https://www.britannica.com/topic/ alcoholic-beverage. Accessed May 7, 2024.

"Children: The Silent Victims of Parental Alcoholism and Substance Use." Brook Lane.org, https://www.brooklane.org/blog/children-silent-victims -parental-alcoholism-substance-use. Accessed February 1, 2024.

"Drinking Too Much Alcohol Can Harm Your Health." Centers for Disease Control and Prevention, published 2022, https://www.cdc.gov/alcohol/ fact-sheets/alcohol-use.htm. Accessed May 9, 2024.

"Eugene O'Neill: Facts." The Nobel Prize.org. https://www.nobelprize.org/ prizes/literature/1936/oneill/facts/. Accessed February 19, 2024.

Fernández, Alexia. "Demi Moore Says Her 'Addiction' to Ashton Kutcher Was 'Devastating': 'It Took Me Away Emotionally.'" *People*, November 4, 2019. https://people.com/movies/demi-moore-addiction-ashton-kutcher -was-devastating/#inbox/_blank. Accessed May 29, 2024.

George, Erin L., MFT. "What Happens to Children of Alcoholic Parents?" MentalHelp.net. https://www.mentalhelp.net/parenting/what-happens -to-children-of-alcoholic-parents/. Accessed February 1, 2024.

Gigliotti, Jim. *Who Was Ernest Hemingway?* New York: Penguin Random House, 2022.

Harmata, Claudia. "Carol Burnett's Tragic History with Addiction in the Family: 'You Can't Cure Them.'" *People*, August 20, 2010. https://people .com/tv/carol-burnett-history-with-addiction-in-the-family/. Accessed April 7, 2024.

Lipari, Rachel. N., and Struther L. Van Horn. *Children Living with Parents Who Have a Substance Use Disorder*. Center for Behavioral Health Statistics and Quality (CBHSQ) report, August 24, 2017. 2017 [cited December 8, 2020]. https://www.samhsa.gov/data/sites/default/files/report_3223/ ShortReport-3223.html. Accessed February 1, 2024.

Maldonado, Lizmarie. "Alcoholism Statistics and Important Facts," American Addiction Center ProjectKnow.com, last updated November 1, 2023, https://projectknow.com/alcohol/statistics/. Accessed February 1, 2024.

McEvoy, Colin. "Jamie Lee Curtis." *Biography*, last updated March 29, 2024. https://www.biography.com/actors/jamie-lee-curtis#inbox/_blank. Accessed February 19, 2024.

"More than 7 Million Children Live with a Parent with Alcohol Problems." *Data Spotlight*, February 16, 2012. Center for Behavioral Health Statistics and Quality. https://www.samhsa.gov/data/sites/default/files/Spot061 ChildrenOfAlcoholics2012/Spot061ChildrenOfAlcoholics2012.pdf. Accessed February 1, 2024.

Mosel, Stacy. "Children of Alcoholics: Growing Up with an Alcoholic Parent." American Addiction Centers, last updated June 18, 2024. https://america naddictioncenters.org/alcohol/support-recovery/child. Accessed February 1, 2024.

"Overview of Alcohol Consumption." National Institute on Alcohol Abuse and Alcoholism. https://www.niaaa.nih.gov/alcohols-effects-health/overview -alcohol-consumption. Accessed May 8, 2024.

Pineda, Dorany. "Ben Affleck Opens Up About Alcohol Addiction, Depression and His Biggest Disappointment." *Los Angeles Times*, February 20, 2020. https://www.latimes.com/entertainment-arts/movies/story/2020-02-20/ ben-affleck-alcohol-addiction-depression-disappointment#inbox/_blank. Accessed April 7, 2024.

Plant, M. A., J. Orford, and M. Grant. "The Effects on Children and Adolescents of Parents' Excessive Drinking: An International Review."

Public Health Report 104, no. 5 (1989): 433–42. Accessed March 5 2024 https://www.ncbi.nlm.nih.gov/pmc/articles/PMC1579958/#:~:text=Problem%20drinking%20by%20a%20parent,of%20psychological%20and%20behavioral%20disorders.

Reich, Wendy. "Prospective Studies of Children of Alcoholic Parents." *Alcohol Health Research World* 21, no. 3 (1997): 255–57. https://www.ncbi.nlm.nih.gov/pmc/articles/PMC6826816/#:~:text=Alcoholism%20tends%20to%20run%20in,Cotton%201979%3B%20Merikangas%20et%20al. Accessed February 1, 2024.

Shewfelt, Raechal. "As Colin Farrell Returns to Rehab, We Look Back at What He's Said about Addiction." *Yahoo Entertainment*, April 4, 2018. https://www.yahoo.com/entertainment/colin-farrell-returns-rehab-look-back-hes-said-addiction-224134118.html. Accessed May 30, 2024.

"Take the ACEs Quiz." American Society for the Positive Care of Children (SPCC). https://americanspcc.org/take-the-aces-quiz/. Accessed May 24, 2024.

Tauber, Michelle. "How Robin Williams Fought, and Lost, His Battles with Addiction and Depression." *People*, August 13, 2014. https://people.com/celebrity/how-robin-williams-fought-and-lost-his-battles-with-addiction-and-depression/. Accessed May 7, 2024.

Teeman, Tim. "Like Father Like Son." *Irish Examiner*, June 16, 2012. https://www.irishexaminer.com/lifestyle/celebrity/arid-20197561.html#inbox/_blank. Accessed April 7, 2024.

"Tony Curtis." *Biography*, last updated April 12, 2021. https://www.biography.com/actors/tony-curtis. Accessed February 19, 2024.

"Understanding Alcohol Use Disorder." National Institute on Alcohol Abuse and Alcoholism, last updated July 2024. https://www.niaaa.nih.gov/publications/brochures-and-fact-sheets/understanding-alcohol-use-disorder. Accessed May 8, 2024.

INDEX

About the Author

Michelle Shreeve is the traditionally published author of *Coping with Parental Death: Insights and Tips for Teenagers* from Rowman & Littlefield's Empowering You series; and *Parental Death: The Ultimate Teen Guide*, also with Rowman & Littlefield from their It Happened to Me series. She has been a freelance writer for the past fifteen years, during which her work has been published both locally and nationally. She is a former newspaper columnist, having written an advice column for almost a decade, and has written journalism pieces, movie reviews, book reviews, academic pieces, repurposed articles, children's fiction stories, fiction auto-ethnographic pieces, and more for newspapers, magazines, and websites.

Shreeve holds two master's degrees, one in English and one in creative writing, and two undergraduate degrees in psychology. She has a library, education, writing, and marketing background and likes to help youth, especially through the power of the written word. She can be reached at michelleshreeveauthor@gmail.com.